> Carol
> Thank you for being with me — you make me better. Always.
> Anderson

Creating Matters:

Reflections on Art, Business, and Life
(so far)

Anderson W. Williams

Carol,
Thanks for creating
with me and making
me better. Always.

Hudson

For Charlie and Zoe: that you will create what it means to be you and share it with the world.

ACKNOWLEDGEMENTS

I first have to thank my parents for believing in something greater and being convicted enough to raise my siblings and me how they did, where they did, when they did. Thanks to Katie, Charlie, and Zoe for your love, understanding, and patience with me as we create our lives together. Thanks to my brother Charlie for the conversation 13 years ago that became this book, and for the continuing dialogue and coffee that have helped shape it. Thanks to my sister Annie B. for the boundless support and encouragement. Thanks to all of my art teachers along the way who gave me the tools and the processes to understand and express my world. Thanks to countless other teachers, coaches, friends, and colleagues who have challenged my thinking, pushed me to be better, and exposed me to new perspectives. Specifically, thank you to Terry Pickeral for being my colleague and critical friend and for being the one who encouraged me to start writing.

TABLE OF CONTENTS

OPENING   **10**
    Introduction   10
    Put a Bucket on Your Head   15
    Learning to Walk   18

PART I: BECOMING   **23**
    I is a Process   26
    We Don't Need Control   29
    Nonviolence   31
    Who or What is an Artist?   39
    Artist as Entrepreneur   49
    Destroy Something You Made   62

PART II: SEEING   **67**
    People and Places   68
    The Whole   80
    Your Work and Career   87
    Craft Your Own Narrative   91
    Life   101

PART III: CREATING   **105**
    Questioning   111
    A Question of Questions   112
    Organizations   115
    The Policy Lobotomy   119
    Creative Tension   122
    Comfort, Risk, Danger   132

Startup Tension 135
A Relational Tension Model 139
Creative vs. Destructive Tension 150
Marriage 153
Creative Leadership 155

CLOSING 165

"Every day we slaughter our finest impulses. That is why we get a heartache when we read those lines written by the hand of the master and recognize them as our own, as the tender shoots which we stifled because we lacked the faith to believe in our own powers, our own criterion of truth and beauty. Every man, when he gets quiet, when he becomes desperately honest with himself, is capable of uttering profound truths. We all derive from the same source. There is no mystery about the origin of things. We are all part of the creation, all kings, all poets, all musicians; we have only to open up, only to discover what is already there." – Henry Miller[1]

"If the artist, or poet, or musician, or dramatist, or philosopher seems somewhat unorthodox in his manner and attitudes, it is because he knows… that orthodoxy has destroyed a great deal of human good, whether of charity, or of good sense, or of art." – Ben Shahn[2]

---

[1] Barron, Frank. *Creators on Creating: Awakening and Cultivating the Imaginative Mind.* New York: Putnam, 1997. 30 Print.
[2] Shahn, Ben. *The Shape of Content.* Cambridge: Harvard UP, 1957. 23. Print.

OPENING

"I force myself to contradict myself in order to avoid conforming to my own taste." - Marcel Duchamp

Introduction

On one of my first days of business school, my professor was facilitating get-to-know-you discussions related to the results of some sort of "brain dominance" test we had all had taken. We all know the tests: the ones that tell you how you think, explain to you in neat paragraphs what that means for you and your leadership, your behaviors in times of stress, and even your personal relationships. They provide a tidy answer for a messy and complicated and "mediumistic" self, as Duchamp characterized it.

As the on-scholarship, head-shaved, goateed, casually dressed, nonprofit "executive" with an MFA, my falling into the creative or "artist" category with such a test was not much of a surprise to anyone. It fulfilled everyone's assumptions, and put me neatly in a category: the "different-than-the-rest-of-us" category.

A decade prior, I had taken a similar test in my first weeks of art school. Ironically, I was the only person in my department of 15 people who was categorized as an "artist" by this particular test. For Cranbrook Academy of Art, or at least my particular department, this was not exactly a badge of belonging. Of course, the reason it's ironic is that I was the student there with the least art experience. As a then clean-cut, sports-watching, former athlete from a liberal arts college in the South, I was the least likely to be identified as the artist of the group by most of the world. It defied most people's assumptions and put me neatly in the "different-than-the-rest-of-us" category.

On the surface, I didn't fit in in either place: art school or business school. Perhaps that's proof that, as an artist, I actually belonged in both. In each case, I thrived on the dissonance. It motivated me. It made me more creative.

In the 10 years between art and business school, I spent 4 years as a community organizer, working with youth in low-wealth neighborhoods and schools to advocate for educational equity and economic justice. I spent a year managing this same organization and then moved to helping other organizations, schools, and cities around the country and internationally engage their young people more strategically and effectively. I have been a consultant on education and youth issues for many years.

While in business school, I helped start the Tennessee College Access and Success Network. And, after a year and a half as the director of strategy there, I left to co-found Zeumo, an education technology startup, which pivoted a year later into healthcare (a field notably absent from my resume to that point).

During the same 10 years, I got married, bought and sold two houses, lost my father to suicide, got a dog, had two daughters, and then moved with my wife and girls back to the house where I grew up, and where my Mom still lives with us.

I taught college-level art for 4 years adjunct.
I stopped doing any studio artwork for 3 years.
I started writing.
I started making art again.
I had my first solo art exhibition, and then my second 10 years later.
I co-founded my first company in education technology and ended up part of a publicly traded healthcare company.

It's been a strange ride, but such is life. I have learned that I am driven by contradiction, not for the sake of it, but for the challenge and the learning, for the dissonance and dynamism. The creativity. For the life of it.

Through it all, I have never lost what Einstein called the "irresistible urge" of the artist to create. I still always see myself as an artist in a studio, if not in the studio. I have created perpetually and in many mediums, in many kinds of studios, and my art, at times, has simply been my life.

Writing, in particular, has become a creative outlet for me over the last few years, so I figured maybe I could/should challenge myself to write a book. Something tells me that if you have chosen to read this you may have had a similar thought about writing or just creating something, anything. If you create frequently in any medium, I suspect you also frequently wonder how to take it to the next level. What's the next challenge? Learning curve? What will force me to get better?

I also think a lot, probably too much, and probably about too many things. So, I wondered if I could force myself to focus on one thing for a while: what it means for me to be an artist, and how that has played out across all facets of my life. It's something I get asked about quite frequently.

In these pages, at the most basic level, I am attempting not to "slaughter" those impulses to write, to create, to reflect and learn from my own experiences, and to share them with you. Hopefully, I won't slaughter your expectations of this book in the process!

Finally, I read a ton (or, at least, did before I had kids) and typically keep a pen in hand to mark passages and pages I think someday I might want to come back to. I have been doing this with almost every book I have read for 15 years. I have never exactly known why or when I would come back, or what I would do with it all. But, it seemed a waste not to mark the books for future reference. I rarely re-read books and my memory is terrible.

So, I developed a system for my markings: underlines for specific quotes, full brackets along the margin for really strong passages that are rich and potentially quotable, but too long to underline, and finally corner brackets to mark the lines that begin and end a passage that I find compelling, but isn't really quote-worthy. It's my process and a modest attempt to organize volumes of reading, markers in my personal exploration.

Most of the passages you will find referenced here come from those marks in business books, fiction, pop psychology, art, organizational studies, leadership, and economics. The common thread among the disparate books and fields they represent is simply my curiosity and the fact that I read them as part of my creative journey. In many cases, references in one good book led to reading two more in a sort of iterative bibliography, one book literally leading to the next. In other cases, I grabbed the obscure and random. However I have found them, I have quoted my readings generously here that you might find a good book to read on the next step of your journey.

All of these books and their ideas are raw material for my own repurposing, my own development. They are not fact. They mostly provide frames of reference with the author's supporting analysis. Or, at least, that's how I read them. I am not looking for answers. I am looking for understanding. I am looking for patterns of thinking and analysis that might inform my own – whether through outright rejection or some level of cooption, or anywhere in between. I am looking for more questions.

So, this book is also not fact and holds no answers and clearly borrows liberally from the good thinking of others. Hopefully, it at least holds some questions and some patterns of thinking that you might choose to riff on in your own exploration. Perhaps you will reject some outright. Regardless, I hope I can offer something here to help you claim your "finest impulses" and find faith in your own process of creating in this world, whatever you create.

Put a Bucket on Your Head

In the July 19, 2010 issue, Newsweek launched the cover story "The Creativity Crisis"[3] by Po Bronson and Ashley Merryman. The article's central concern is research demonstrating that American creativity is on the decline and has been since 1990. The article also specifies that: "It is the scores of younger children in America – from kindergarten through sixth grade – for whom the decline is 'most serious.'" I read the article both disturbed by its premise and hopeful for its possibility (we know creativity can be more effectively cultivated and taught if we choose to make such a commitment).

Not long after I read the article, I went on family vacation where I got to relax on the beach with about 30 family members and family friends, about a half-dozen of whom fell into that "most serious" category for creative decline, sixth grade or below. Even as I sit at the beach with them every year and seemingly do nothing more than read for hours at a time (again, this was more true before I had kids of my own), I always receive incredible energy from the spirit and play of my younger nieces and cousins, and now my own daughters. On this particular trip, however, my then 5-year-old niece also gave me a little refresher course on creativity, as well as a powerful reminder that we need to understand creativity not as something exclusive to art or art-making (what the Newsweek article refers to as the "art bias") but as an approach to navigating our world and our relationships.

---

[3] http://www.newsweek.com/creativity-crisis-74665

After a couple of days of self-driven play in the water and in the sand with her cousins, her sister, her parents, and her grandparents, my niece was still exploring the world around her, still seeking to understand her relationship to it. She did this not by seeking or taking advice on how to build a "good" sandcastle; not by asking her older cousins to introduce her to a new game; not by proclaiming boredom and asking what she could do now; she did it by putting a bucket on her head.

She didn't ask if it was OK to put a bucket on her head; she just did it (of course begging the question of whether it should still be considered a bucket at this point).

She didn't put the bucket on her head and parade around to show everyone else how funny she was; she did it for herself.

She didn't even put the bucket on her head to pretend it was a hat; she just put a bucket on her head.

And, without seeking any attention, she began exploring her new "bucket-head" relationship with the sand and the experience of digging in the sand. Having re-explored digging, she moved to the water's edge and tried walking in the waves and filling another bucket with water while maintaining the first bucket's position covering her head and face completely. With this new world of water more deeply understood, she tried interacting with her cousins to understand what it would be like to be a "bucket-head" cousin. With a bucket on her head, she re-experienced it all! And, she was the ONLY person on the beach who knew that unique and "divergent" experience. The rest of us just sat there; and the sand was the sand and the water was the water and cousins were cousins.

According to the Newsweek article, "Creativity requires constant shifting, blender pulses of both divergent thinking and convergent thinking, to combine new information with old and forgotten ideas." Putting a bucket on her head was my niece's first move to "shift" the world around her and to solicit new and divergent perspectives from the world she already knew. To the credit of the rest of the family, no one imposed convergent thought on her by telling her a bucket "didn't belong" on her head. She was allowed to create and process her own new experiences. It was beautiful. It was profound. It was innate.

Creativity is part of what it means to be a child. Imagining and creating relationships, conjuring games, living unaware of others' critical eyes, children are the natural spring well of human creativity. So, how have we as a country managed to decline in creativity for the last 20 years? And, how is it even conceivable that it is even more in decline with our children? (The authors lay the story out far better than anything I can offer and I highly suggest reading the article for their analysis and thoughtful perspective.)

We all know the detrimental implications on our economy and our "global competitiveness" when we see such a decline in creativity. This economic impact, framed by a creativity decline or myriad other issues, is almost always forefront in our political media. What isn't talked about much is the detrimental impact on our day-to-day lives, our personal and professional relationships, even our democracy. Creativity, or the lack thereof, impacts every aspect of our selves and our society.

We cannot afford to forget that our economy, our democracy, like creativity, like art, like our selves, describe processes, not facts. We cannot afford to smother or otherwise let atrophy this process that was once innate and core to our childhood being. We cannot "slaughter" it. This must be our challenge as adults for ourselves and our young people. In the words of Ken Robinson: "I believe profoundly that we don't grow into creativity; we grow out of it."[4]

Learning to Walk

With this in mind, it is probably worth making the connection between creativity and learning. The former cannot exist without the latter. Learning is the ultimate creativity of the self.

The last several years of watching my daughters grow and learn and create definitely reinforce Ken Robinson's point that creativity and, by default, learning, are innate. I have now watched two daughters begin and successfully complete the process of learning how to walk, and each time has been truly profound. It's thrilling. It's emotional. In fact, all you really need to know about learning you can learn from a toddler.

---

[4] Robinson, Ken. *Out of Our Minds: Learning to Be Creative*. Fully Rev. and Updated ed. Oxford: Capstone, 2011. 49. Print.

In their efforts, I see something elemental, but that has nothing to do with the physical act of walking. I see something that is at the essence of being and yet, as an act, does little to define them. I see a process unfold that is often considered a skill, but is better understood and encouraged as an awakening; learning that generates more learning.

Toddlers don't have to be convinced to learn to walk. They can obviously be encouraged, but they do it because they want to. It should be noted here that those children with disabilities preventing them from walking will experience and demonstrate this learning in their own way and true to their own abilities. We need to be creative enough to recognize and learn from their creativity too, even if (or perhaps especially if) it takes a different form. With their actions, our children learning to walk can enlighten us about the critical elements of learning:

Curiosity (Internal Motivation)
At some point, while sitting on the carpet in our living room, my daughter looks up. She looks up to where my wife and I are sitting, where we put our iPad and the remote control, and yes, where we also put our dinner many nights. She can't see where all this is, but she knows it's up there. Something is up there. And, then one day, she just reaches up.

New Perspectives
She puts her hands on our coffee table and squirms her body vertical, her muscles unsure of their new relation to gravity. She stands, wobbly, looking around. It is clear in her eyes, she is seeing a whole new world – a world from roughly two feet high that shows her things she has never seen before (without our help), and changes her perspective on the things she has.

External Incentives
What is this new world? What is that on the couch? Look at those colors on the pillows! The remote control is fascinating. How can she get it? She wants and needs to explore these objects. She reaches, but her arms are too short. We urge her on with positive messages (and move everything on our coffee table to one side).

Struggle
But, it is all still there and it still tempts her. And yet, she stands; her legs beginning to shake in fatigue, as she knows neither how to move toward the objects nor how to get back to the safety of the floor. She is stuck. Then, one day… the right heel comes off the ground…and then back down. The right knee comes up…but the left one shakes. She cries a moment, unsure. And, suddenly she takes a side step and her hands instinctively shift position to support her along the tabletop.

Reflection
"Hmmm...what just happened? I just moved from there to here. Um...I can do this! That thing I just did with my legs and hands may get me over there to all the stuff I want to explore." Within a couple of days, she masters moving from surface to surface to get around the living room. My wife and I have moved everything to higher ground (and also begin noticing every potential danger in the room).

Experimentation
After a week or so of pulling up and side stepping around the room, one day she stands, right in the middle of the room. She just stands, holding onto nothing. She looks around. My wife and I hold our breaths. She drops, and crawls where she needs to go. But, she keeps doing this again and again as if knowing there is something to it, a new opportunity there, but not sure what it is. Then she stands...a half-step...drop...crawl...

Courage and Resilience
So, one day, one of us holds a favorite toy or book out a few feet from her, and she haltingly and hesitantly starts to wobble forward. One step...and down. She gets back up. One...two...three steps...and down. She gets back up. One...two...three...four steps...and down.

And, she continues her process with modest daily improvements but with a **confidence** that is beginning to surge. The fear and uncertainty that have flooded her countenance begin to shift to a look of **joy and pride** in her efforts and our reinforcement.

And, with every new step, her curiosity is again piqued, her perspective expanded and her learning process gathers inertia. She has learned how to walk. So, what's next?

Learning opens our minds, exposes us to new vantage points, more things to see, to touch, to explore. It is both the source and the result of creativity. Imagine if I carried my daughters' capacity to learn with me everyday as an adult! Imagine what we could do directing all of that learning toward creating our lives and the world we want to live in!

We can. Or, at least we can try. But, first we must commit to being lifelong learners and deploying our learning creatively, as an approach to life, to relationships, a way of seeing the world, of making the world. To be so empowered even as we age, we must defy creativity's degradation as "The Creativity Crisis" describes it. We must transform the default creativity of the child into the discipline of the adult.

PART I:
BECOMING

Years ago, on another annual family beach trip, my wife's uncle gave me a book by philosopher Joseph Pieper that included the insight: "Man is insofar as he becomes."[5]

Needless to say I underlined it, and this is the one passage I have come back to countless times in my personal life and professional development. I used it when I was working with inner-city youth trying to help them think beyond the trappings of their economic status, neighborhood, race, and school. I tried to help them see themselves as a process to be claimed and developed, not as a series of static and oppressive labels applied by others, by history. Instead of asking them who they were, or what they wanted to be or do when they grow up, I asked them who they were becoming.

I asked myself the same thing as I considered the daunting task of graduate school at Cranbrook Academy of Art and then again a decade later at the Owen Graduate School of Management. Who was I becoming when I helped start a nonprofit college access network or co-founded a technology company? Who am I becoming as I write this book? Answering this question was not just about what I was going to "do" next or why, but how it integrated into my larger purpose on this planet. Each was a huge challenge that I had to transform into genuine opportunities.

But lots of things are challenges, and I am privileged to have had lots of opportunities. There had to be something more. I had to understand why I was

---

[5] Pieper, Josef. *Only the Lover Sings: Art and Contemplation*. San Francisco: Ignatius, 1990. Print.

choosing these in particular. What would I learn? What would I face? What would make me uncomfortable? How would all of it relate to the world as I understand it? Increase my understanding? I knew if I couldn't answer these types of questions, that when things got tough, I would get disillusioned and lose motivation. In fact, over the years, this has been the one piece of advice I have given people who were considering applying to Owen or Cranbrook: know why you are there and remind yourself about it when you are struggling. You will struggle.

The question of becoming, however, is far more profound than seizing opportunity. It can also be about pure survival. When my Father committed suicide, I was 30 years old. The world, everything I knew, every relationship, shifted, some subtly, some dramatically. There are months of my life around that time that I don't remember. There are relationships that proved more meaningful than I ever knew. Others proved hollow.

But, who was I? As a son? A brother? A husband? What did it mean to have lost my Dad, to hold him only in memory? What would I do with the gift of the 30 years of being his son? What would I do with his death? Through all of it, who was I becoming? After Dad's death, I had a bucket on my head whether I liked it or not. It was time to reorient and see my world and my self in new terms.

I needed that question of becoming, in many ways, to shock me back into the process of living. I own my brokenness. I own my confusion, my loneliness. But, I also own what I will do with it, what will become of it. Who and what will I become?

I is a Process
And, the beauty of this thinking is that I, my self, become a process. The challenge, however, is also that I become a process.

As a process, I am mutable. I am responsible for myself. I require continuous input, fuel, investment, nutrition, or the process stops. If I am not vigilant and invested, I stagnate, ending up a static being. I am a thing, a concept. If I am a process, on the other hand, I am in flux. I am dynamic. I do not rest. I am never done.

As a result, I can also get tired and overwhelmed, exhausted by too many decisions, interpretations, navigating multiple truths and perceived realities. I can leave myself wondering "how in the hell did I end up here!?" generally followed by "and how am I going to make the most of it?"

While it's all part of my creative energy and process, at times, it can also feel like existential vertigo.

So, to sustain my self in process, as process, it is critical that I cultivate a sense of presence as both an investment in my becoming as well as in maintaining my sanity.

Robert Persig visualizes the process and transition to presence in the classic <u>Zen and the Art of Motorcycle Maintenance</u>: "Mountains should be climbed with as little effort as possible and without desire. The reality of your own nature should determine the speed. If you become restless, speed up. If you become winded, slow down. You climb the mountain in an equilibrium between restlessness and exhaustion. Then, when you're no longer thinking ahead, each footstep isn't just a means to an end but a unique event in itself…It's the sides of the mountain that sustain life, not the top."[6]

It's difficult when you lose something or somebody, or have any significant change in your life for that matter, not to look backward for excuses, explanations, and imagined alternatives. The top of your mountain has changed and you are trying to hold onto it. So, it's also hard not to look forward and obsess on and grasp for the unknown and uncontrollable. So, we struggle for an equilibrium between the two, we try to hold on to that old mountaintop when deep down we know it's not our destination. We falsely believe it is what has sustained us. But, as Persig explains, the real answer we need and want is right here, right now, in the fullness and possibility of the present moment, here on the sides of the mountain. To extend his metaphor further, the struggle between a past (the mountain we have already climbed) and future (the mountaintop) denies the present (mountainside). That struggle is ultimately futile, and it consumes the creative energy we need to remain present and forge a new way forward.

"Soon today becomes the past. You can't hold on. Yet the creative process is a fact of the current moment. You

---

[6] Pirsig, Robert M. *Zen and the Art of Motorcycle Maintenance: An Inquiry into Values*,. New York: Morrow, 1974. 258. Print.

can't go back in the past and create. And while you can prepare for the future now, you can't reach into the future and create. The creative process happens in real time. The orientation that is needed is one in which we can live in the present."[7]

The future is inherently more dynamic than the past will ever be. The past is memory. The future is possibility. The present is life, framed and guided by our interpretation of both past and future.

At one of my lowest points, I read a passage in a book on Buddhism that talked about how humans, as uniquely sentient beings, live a life of suffering. We cannot control this fact. What we can control, what we have power over, however, is whether we struggle. How do we respond to that suffering?

This revelation was both humbling and liberating, and it has challenged me almost every day since. It was pivotal in allowing me to start creating my life again and stop struggling with a past and a future that were and are beyond my grasp and control.

After all, life is mostly unknowns. Even our knowns are mostly perceptions or subject to history's persuasions. Life is mostly uncontrollable, because it is mostly random. "The outline of our lives, like the candle's flame, is continuously coaxed in new directions by a variety of random events that, along with our responses to them, determine our fate. As a result, life is both hard to predict and hard to interpret."[8]

---

[7] Fritz, Robert. *Your Life as Art*. Newfane, VT: Newfane, 2003. 20. Print.
[8] Mlodinow, Leonard. *The Drunkard's Walk: How Randomness Rules Our Lives*. New York: Pantheon, 2008. 4. Print.

But, we want to predict, we want clear interpretations, we want control. We think we need control. We think it's the only way to stay "sane" in a complex and dynamic world. In reality, this struggle for control exacerbates and prolongs our suffering.

We Don't Need Control

We have misunderstood our needs. We have misapplied the idea of control and invested massive amounts of energy in controlling things that aren't meaningful, or are not even controllable. We have done so because we have sought control for control's sake. We have merged the ideas of control and power and comfort. We have sought to control symptoms to compensate for our perceived lack of control of systems and root causes. We have sought control for control's sake.

The idea of control is too often about things we never will, or about things that won't actually get us what we want. But, control makes us feel powerful when we are weak, temporarily more together when we feel most scattered. It obscures systemic flaws in our relationships or our approach to work and life. Control is typically a cover. It is temporary relief. But, lack of control is often the only problem we are trying to solve with control. In other words, control itself actually becomes the goal – not the resolution of the source issue. As such, it reinforces our futile struggle to avoid suffering, creating more suffering in an endless spiral.

But, the need for control isn't always false and it doesn't have to be fringe or futile. There is something fundamentally human to it. We just need to tweak our understanding a bit to make it work for us. We must begin to understand and assess our lives and our surroundings in terms of controllable variables. In fact, part of being present depends on our ability to see the controllable variables in our lives and relationships, moment-to-moment and long term. Controllable, in this sense, doesn't mean we have the variables that make up our lives and our surroundings under control, or even in control. Instead, it means that first we recognize what is a variable and then identify which of those are impacted in meaningful ways by our everyday choices and actions. Controllable variables are those that we can create upon.

When we act with an analysis of the variables we can control, we act with a sense of purpose about a larger goal, rooted in a deeper understanding of ourselves and the world - all variables, some controllable. In this way, we allow ourselves the opportunity move beyond a problem-solving mentality, chronically stuck in the frustration and blame and powerlessness of uncontrollable variables, and into creative living.

"We have been trained to think of situations that are inadequate for our aspirations as problems. When we think of them as problems, we try to solve them. When you are solving a problem, you are taking action to have something go away: the problem. When you are creating, you are taking action to have something come into being:

the creation. Notice that the intentions of these actions are opposite."[9]

Robert Fritz continues: "In the tradition of the arts, it is well known that creating is not problem solving. The reason that this distinction is important is that most people are truly interested in creating the lives they want. Problem solving does not enable them to create what they want and often perpetuates what they do not want."

To put it simply, problem solving has a clear, but limited, destination: the anti-problem a.k.a. the solution. It is the presumed offspring of control. But, it is a trap. If we do find a solution, we will face the next problem as if it is unique and seek another solution. Problems and solutions continue to proliferate from a larger broken system, which proves again we aren't actually in control. Because we address them one-by-one, we never see the system. We never see the whole, so, we never seek to create a new reality. We just keep solving problems rather than creating new systems. Think duct tape.

Nonviolence

I had the incredible fortune of meeting Dr. Bernard Lafayette, one of the great Civil Rights leaders of the student-led nonviolent movement in my hometown of Nashville. He and his peers literally changed the world. They integrated lunch counters. They rode Greyhound buses through the heart of the Jim Crow South to

---

[9] Fritz, Robert. *The Path of Least Resistance: Learning to Become the Creative Force in Your Own Life.* Rev. ed. New York: Ballantine, 1989. 11, 41. Print.

integrate bus stations. They were beaten. Bombed. Imprisoned. They were children. (Note: Please read David Halberstam's book The Children.) They were not solving a problem. They were creating the future for all of us.

Because he was just a youth during this time, Dr. Lafayette knew how important it was to take time to talk with my young people working with Community IMPACT, who were trying to change their schools and their neighborhoods: places of violence, joblessness, poverty, and lack of educational opportunity. And, as you might expect, he talked to them about nonviolence. Without understanding and embracing and practicing the discipline of nonviolence, he told them, they would struggle to change anything systemically.

You can imagine the response and confusion of young people whose lives were surrounded by violence, who were shown every day that defeating your enemy, rather than getting them to join you, was success. Being more violent, or the most violent, or aligning with those who are, was the only way many knew to stay safe. The kid who joined a gang for protection. The kid raped by a drug dealer. The kid who saw a friend and schoolmate get shot in her front yard. The kids who had tear gas dropped in the hallway of their school. The kid scared to death of the school's police officer. I could go on.

Nonviolence met the same skepticism it has met in almost all oppressed communities seeking relief, seeking solutions, seeking some control. It was too passive.

Counterintuitive. But, nonviolence can only be understood as a creative force.

My young people asked Dr. Lafayette a lot of questions. They sought clarification. They listened with guarded skepticism, still offering a degree of reverence for the man who sat before them and all he had accomplished - for them. But, maybe he was just "old school" and a little crazy now in his older age. This nonviolence stuff might have worked back then, but today was different.

And then, Dr. Lafayette said three words that transformed the conversation, and the understanding of the world by my youth and me: "Revenge is endless."

After a bit of silence, you could see the lights going on in the young minds around the table (and mine). That actually made sense!

Revenge, the revengeful act, is defined and controlled by the initial transgression. It doubles down on it. Validates it. Gives it power. And, we return to it because it feels like a way to solve a problem, to regain control of a situation. But, it never is. Or, it is only temporary and our revenging actions are eventually revenged in an endless loop. My young people knew this loop. They lived it. But, to move beyond the intuitive act of revenge, to buy into this understanding of nonviolence at a deep level requires a thorough understanding of systems. We have be able to locate ourselves and the opposing person or issue in a context. We have to have the discipline to think and work and act systemically.

We barely scratched the surface, but we did continue to explore nonviolence together after our time with Dr. Lafayette and discovered some key principles to study and to reflect on in our own efforts. Two of these principles really illuminate the creativity of nonviolence, the focus on creating more just communities rather than solving each injustice on its own, much less avenging them:

Nonviolence seeks to win friendship and understanding.[10] *The end result of nonviolence is redemption and reconciliation. The purpose of nonviolence is the creation of the Beloved Community.*

Nonviolence seeks to defeat injustice not people.
Nonviolence recognizes that evildoers are also victims and are not evil people. The nonviolent resister seeks to defeat evil not people.

The first principle realizes that to transform conditions we must first develop relationships. Most importantly, we must create them where they have not existed, where they were determined never to exist.

The second recognizes the systemic nature, the connectedness, of all of us. It takes the emphasis off of the evildoer, the one most of us seek revenge upon, and understands he is a victim as well. In our work, we must create a just world for all of us.

---

[10] http://www.thekingcenter.org/king-philosophy#sub2

Both of these principles rely on a deeper understanding of our humanity, of the relationship between struggle and suffering, which is illuminated in another principle of nonviolence:

Nonviolence holds that suffering can educate and transform. *Nonviolence accepts suffering without retaliation. Unearned suffering is redemptive and has tremendous educational and transforming possibilities.*

In other words, if we deny our suffering and instead invest our energy in struggling against it, we will lose its learning and its redemption.

So, if we buy in to this philosophy in our everyday lives, how can we be more present with our suffering in a way that alleviates some of the struggle? How can we relinquish control in a way that actually allows us to create? How can we create rather than always problem solve? How can we focus on the process of becoming and yet be fully present with what is happening to us, with us, around us?

Like the principles of nonviolent revolution, the relationship between suffering and struggle, between creating and problem-solving, between process and presence at times feel contradictory, and at others even redundant - which in itself seems contradictory!

In fact, they relate in a more dynamic interpretation of the world, and a deeper philosophy of our role in it, than we typically allow in our everyday lives. They are drivers of a non-linear world, a world that is also becoming, and we are creating as we become within it.

"Because the actual world, that in which we live, is a combination of movement and culmination, of breaks and re-unions, the experience of a living creature is capable of esthetic quality. The live being recurrently loses and reestablishes equilibrium with his surroundings. The moment of passage from disturbance into harmony is that of intensest life. In a finished world, sleep and waking could not be distinguished. In one wholly perturbed, conditions could not even be struggled with. In a world made after the pattern of ours, moments of fulfillment punctuate experience with rhythmically enjoyed intervals."[11]

Expanding in some ways on this analysis by John Dewey, quantum physics shows us an entirely new world of life in which things exist only inasmuch as they have relationships with other things. With this perspective, living becomes a constant process of connecting, disconnecting, and interacting. It recalls the nonviolent principle of winning friends as part of creating the more just and equitable world we desire. The relationship is fundamental. In her extraordinary book Leadership and the New Science, Margaret Wheatley translates a bit of the quantum worldview for the consumption of non-scientist readers like me: "We live in a universe where relationships are primary. Nothing happens in the quantum world without something encountering something else. Nothing exists

---

[11] Dewey, John. *Art as Experience*. New York: Perigee Books, 1980. 16. Print.

independent of its relationships. We are constantly creating the world – evoking it from many potentials – as we participate in all its many interactions. This is a world of process, the process of connecting, where "things" come into temporary existence because of relationship."

Again, if it sounds contradictory, it kind of is – or, at least, paradoxical. Wheatley continues: "In much of new science, we are challenged by paradoxical concepts – matter that is immaterial, disequilibrium that leads to stability, and now chaos that is ordered. It is chaos' great destructive energy that dissolves the past and gives us the gift of a new future…Only chaos creates the abyss in which we can recreate ourselves."[12]

And, it is in relation to this process of creation and recreation of himself and his relationship with the world that the artist emerges, applies his creativity toward "a new future," toward himself becoming.

I create my art in all of its forms to create new relationships with myself, with the world around me, with my own ideas. They, in turn, create me. I don't create to control the chaos of my mind or my world but to build on its "many potentials" creating and crafting new realities among the relationships that are most important and most alive to me.

Artists exist because of art, which exists because of artists, a world of process and quantum relationships. "The (art) work… also speaks, and at times it is the artist

---

[12] Wheatley, Margaret J. *Leadership and the New Science: Learning about Organization from an Orderly Universe.* San Francisco: Berrett-Koehler, 1992. 69, 119. Print.

who listens. The work in progress begins to look more like a conversation than a lecture."[13] Relationship.

And, when we share our work with an audience, with the world, we invite others into the process of creation, of meaning, of our own becoming. So, art exists not just because of its relationship to the artist but to the audience as well. It is co-created. This is a particularly hard lesson to learn as a young artist. Starting out, we often struggle with illusions of our own grand thoughts and our infallible attempts to communicate them. We believe that the act of making something is what makes us an artist. And, if the audience doesn't "get" it, then it's their fault. This is often the source of intellectual elitism in the arts and is a practice that misunderstands the relational existence of things. If you can't build that relationship with a viewer, can you claim you have created something real?

Quantum mechanics continues to explain this relational reality between the observer and the observed: "At atomic and sub-atomic levels, quantum theory indicates "the inseparability of the observing instrument and that which is being observed": the observing process actively affects that which is being observed, generating a conundrum of meaning that makes it ever more difficult to assume that any description objectively corresponds with "reality."[14]

While I have known many artists over the years who would fundamentally disagree with me, who believe the

---
[13] Eisner, Elliot W. *The Arts and the Creation of Mind.* New Haven: Yale UP, 2002. 78. Print.
[14] Bohm, David, and Lee Nichol. *On Creativity.* London: Routledge, 1998. XX. Print.

artist's intention is the only reality, most of them live in a level of creative isolation that suggests they may be wrong. Additionally, I suspect few of them could imagine a leader without followers, a speaker without listeners, a doctor without patients, a servant without those to be served. The cult of the artist as individual, isolated genius is a self-limiting delusion that denies the relational reality of the creative world.

Who or What is an Artist?

I have never known anyone for whom his art was so much his life and his purpose than my college printmaking professor David Faber. And, while he may be disappointed that I did not become a printmaker in his footsteps, he should know that his craft and his teaching were a lightening rod and a validation for the art I try to live today, in this writing, in my studio art, in my work, and in my relationship with the world. He, more than anyone, introduced to me the process of art making, the relationship among art, artist, medium, and viewer.

David liked to talk about synesthesia as he walked us through various traditional printmaking processes. He taught us to pay attention to the smell of the ink and the mineral spirits, to feel the smoothness of a fresh zinc plate or clean press bed, to hear the pop of ink being mixed with the knife and to tune the smack of a properly inked brayer, to appreciate the richness of good paper and to find the rhythm and balance in wiping an intaglio plate. Feel the time. Become the process. Revel in the result.

It was all there. (It makes me emotional just in reflection and I haven't pulled a print with David in 15 years.) His reverence, his sense of purpose, process. His teaching. He praised and prodded. Challenged and encouraged. Shared excitement and wonder. He was still learning – not about printmaking as a process, but as a unique tool of creation, of self, for each of his students. Art was life.

What could we do with it? What would we do with it?

In graduate school, my department head Steve Murakishi approached things quite a bit differently. He was cynical. He was cryptic, often acerbic. "Irony is dead." Art was about the idea, the communication. He sparred intellectually with us, with the world, not merely as gamesmanship but as a test of meddle. He was a master at creating a void and pushing you into it. And, he would never throw you a rope to get out, no matter how much you tried and struggled. As an artist, that was your personal charge. Toughen up. Get smart. Be relevant. Art was life.

What could we do with it? What would we do with it?

Again, these two artists could not be more different. In fact, I suspect by their nature and the intensity of their purpose and process, they could probably barely stand to be in the same room together.

Navigating their contradictions is not about what is right or wrong, better or worse, contemporary or historical, relevant or irrelevant, artist or not. Their contradiction is art. And, if we leave it as such rather than position ourselves behind ideology or judgment, one or the other, we can challenge ourselves with the values of both. We can use it to stay in constant motion, learning, acknowledging our own preferences and contradictions and using them as fuel to evolve our selves. Becoming.

But, despite their differences, David and Steve are still examples of artists that fall under the traditional definition of artist. They work in studios. They make stuff. They put it out in galleries or public spaces for other to enjoy, critique, and interact with. And, for most people, this is the picture of what an artist is. This is the definition.

And, ironically, most people I have worked with in youth work or education or even in starting a business have no idea that I am an artist – at least by that definition. When they find out, they often expect I am really good at "drawing" for example. I am not. What they do not realize is that in my every interaction with them, whether informal in conversation or structured in facilitation, I am an artist and employing the tools and thought processes I learned from Faber, Murakishi and many others along the way.

I don't know how many times over the years I have had people tell me how "un-artistic" they are. This is probably the most common response when people find out that I'm an artist. "Oh, really!? I'm a terrible artist!" I heard it when I worked with youth doing something as simple as making a poster, or with teachers whom I asked to draw what success looks like for their students. It could be with executives asked to draw their organizational culture without using any words. "I can't do this. I'm a terrible artist."

And, while many of them, in fact, were terrible artists, it had nothing to do with their ability to draw. It had to do with self-imposed limitations to their thinking, professionally imposed containers for their growth and development, arbitrary cultural and social boundaries and definitions of who they are and how they relate to the world. And, it was based on how all of these things established their expectations and evaluation of themselves.

In other words, if they were "bad artists," it was because as black youth they bought into what they were told it meant to be a black youth rather than seeking ways to defy it and create their own identity. They were "bad artists" because as teachers they accepted what they were told a teacher was supposed to be rather than creating effective and engaging learning environments based on what they knew about their students and their own strengths as educators. "Bad artists" mistake their job title as their professional identity, as something to do rather than an environment to own and create and model for others.

Years ago, I was doing work with my colleague Terry Pickeral in Trinidad and Tobago with the Ministries of Education and Local Government. During a week of training, we offered a group of educators there the prompt to draw the culture of their school. I will never forget, because it got Terry and me laughing too, how one group nervously giggled for probably 20 minutes as they first began navigating the prompt. You would have thought that they were middle schoolers we had asked to discuss the reproductive process. They were so uncomfortable!

The beauty was that they knew their reaction was part of the learning of the process. They were more self aware than most groups we've worked with. The group ultimately created their picture and as they presented to their colleagues laughed hysterically and had the whole group laughing along with them. And, while the laughing was a way of coping with their "lack" of skills as an artist, it did remind Terry and me that if we are going to create together, we probably should laugh together a little more often. Laughing had helped them open up. It had helped them relate to each other and the ideas they were trying to draw. Laughing was part of their art. It was a manifestation of their humility.

On another occasion, we tried a similar process with a different prompt with teachers and staff at an alternative school, a school for kids who had been kicked out of the schools they were "supposed" to be attending. For this scenario, we asked a group of teachers to draw two images: 1. a picture of the student when s/he arrived in their school, and 2. a picture of the successful student who left their school ready to return to their original school.

Some of the teachers dove right in and visually represented their versions of confidence, academic improvement, discipline, and new relationships and trust. They drew pictures of the things they sought to instill in the students. But, others struggled as they attempted to draw images of the problems they were trying to solve. How do they draw the absence of bad behavior? How do you draw a kid not failing? Not fighting? They were trapped in the problem-solving frame. That's what kept them from being artists.

As facilitators, we were presented the opportunity to have a powerful conversation with this small group of teachers about purpose and vision and creativity. We were able to surface cracks in consistency among practices and philosophies, cracks students were falling into. We were able to demonstrate to leadership that work was needed to create the environment that supported creativity rather than the traditional command-and-control model for such schools. For example, we had to have a discussion about goals related to discipline as compulsion versus discipline involving the choices of the student. And, of course, we had to talk about relationships among staff, among students, and among staff and students.

Every time I have used this protocol, it has helped people have conversations they have never had before, to see things a little differently. All of these young people and adults over the years, all of these "terrible artists" through a simple prompt took a small step toward returning to creativity. These are steps we can all take, regardless of where or how or with whom we work. "The desire to create is not limited by beliefs, nationality, creed, educational background or era. Your involvement in this (artistic) tradition (is) not limited to the arts, but can encompass all of your life, from the mundane to the profound".[15]

To take this step, however, to reconnect with this desire, can feel risky. That's why that group in Trinidad was laughing so!

Wait, you want me to make what?

I can't use words?

You want me to imagine what? And draw it?

And, I have to stand up and present it to my peers?

We use the protocol because we know that creating is risky. Being an artist is risky. Becoming our best selves is risky.

Not to mention, sometimes it's just fun to watch adults squirm! Most importantly though, it's critical to help adults reflect on why we are squirming, why we are so uncomfortable with such a simple task. For teachers, we are putting them in the position of their students. For bosses, we are putting them in the position of their staff. For community leaders, we are putting them in the position of those who they are asking to follow them. Why is that uncomfortable, and why does that risk matter to what they are trying to accomplish in their work?

To be an artist means finding, embracing, and sustaining an element of risk in our lives, relationships,

---

[15] Fritz, Robert. *The Path of Least Resistance: Learning to Become the Creative Force in Your Own Life*. Rev. ed. New York: Ballantine, 1989. 13. Print.

and daily experiences. The process of creating holds an innate risk that the artist can never escape.

So, an artist is an entrepreneur that imagines and then works to create a new way of supporting critically ill cancer patients and caring for their caretakers in the last weeks and days of life.

An artist is a teacher who uses class time to create environments that provoke curiosity and confusion – an absence of answers – to support the process of learning rather than just delivering an education.

An artist is a nonprofit leader who finds innovative ways to serve her community, engages her people in shared ownership of the work, creates new funding mechanisms to increase sustainability.

An artist is a young person who decides he is more than his school and community says he is, who advocates and organizes for himself and others to access the same opportunities automatically afforded to peers of a different color or class or part of town.

And, yes, an artist is a creator who with the stroke of a brush, the turn of a phrase, the sculpting of materials moves us, provokes us, inspires us, and gives us pause to help us see and reflect on the world around us.

Art is all of it. And, while I do believe in art, visual, performing, and so forth, in the traditional sense, I think distinguishing it from a broader world of artists only isolates the traditional arts, and weakens their connection to the broader culture. Art is a unique capacity and element of what it means to be human, and it is too often obfuscated based on differing forms of creative output rather than understood within the commonality of the creative process.

For most artists and creators, particularly serial creators, the creative process even transcends our humanity. It is spiritual, existential. It is fundamental to exploring and defining and iterating on our selves and our role in the larger world, something rooted within the individual but relevant to the larger human story. From a religious perspective, Pope John Paul II articulated it well: "Not all are called to be artists in the specific sense of the term. Yet, as Genesis has it, all men and women are entrusted with the task of crafting their own life: in a certain sense, they are to make of it a work of art."[16]

Beyond crafting her own life, or perhaps as part of that crafting, an artist is what bell hooks calls an "engaged voice" that "must never be fixed and absolute but always changing, always evolving in dialogue with a world beyond itself."[17] Becoming.

And while both of these terms ("engaged" and "voice") are pretty jargony at this point, there is some value in taking a look at how hooks is using them. The idea of engagement is something that is internal. It is sourced from the level of identity, personal motivation; some might even suggest the soul. Engagement represents a faith in oneself – particularly the faith to question. It is a power and gift we all have if we manage not to "slaughter" it, or allow others to do so. How we engage is our ultimate locus of control, our energy

---

[16] *Letter to Artists*. Chicago, Ill.: Liturgy Training Publications, 1999. 2. Print.
[17] hooks, bell. *Teaching to Transgress: Education as the Practice of Freedom*. New York: Routledge, 1994. 11. Print.

source. It is also a qualifier of our activity, or interactivity, in the world around us. Daniel Kahneman describes it this way: "Those who avoid the sin of intellectual sloth could be called "engaged." They are more alert, more intellectually active, less willing to be satisfied with the superficially attractive answers, more skeptical about their intuitions."[18]

Voice is our resulting expression, our faith in ourselves manifest. It is our celebration and exultation of who we are, what we believe, how we share ourselves with the world, our tool for connecting and affecting beyond ourselves. It is our medium, and one which itself is made of countless mediums and manifestations of our creative acts in the world. It is the presentation of the self to the world.

It is from this dynamic between the internal sense of identity and its relationship and responsibility to a broader world that the artist asks his questions, finds his process, his engagement, and ultimately himself. It is his source of creativity.

What we create, our works, our artworks, our businesses, are all snapshot manifestations of a greater process, a time stamp on our becoming, a milepost on our life's journey. The various forms of artistic output are infinite. The artist makes the medium. The medium doesn't make one an artist.

---

[18] Kahneman, Daniel. *Thinking, Fast and Slow*. New York: Farrar, Straus and Giroux, 2011. 46. Print.

Artist as Entrepreneur

"An experience you don't learn from is just a happening."
- Myles Horton[19]

So, I'll wrap up this section with few reflections on my most recent artistic iteration, becoming an entrepreneur.

I had a business school professor ask me one time why I had been (actually how I had survived being) in nonprofit work for a decade given my interest in entrepreneurship, and the fact that I was in business school. For him, it didn't make sense that I had spent 10 years in "charity" work. (I don't think he even knew of my visual arts background. That would have really confused him!) But, this is a common misperception, a fabricated disconnect, between and among various forms of creativity. The context and the medium get confused as the art. Now, I have plenty of critiques of the lack of creativity in the nonprofit sector, but have learned that the same critiques in the same intensity apply in most any company, school, government organization or otherwise. It's about the human condition and instinct as we organize ourselves in formal groups. But for me, everything I did in 10 years in nonprofit was just as creative, if not more so, than what I have done as an entrepreneur, or as a visual artist for that matter.

In fact, in every position I held for that 10 years, I was creating something new. In many cases, I was not only

---

[19] Horton, Myles, and Judith Kohl. *The Long Haul: An Autobiography*. New York: Doubleday, 1990. 176. Print.

creating (or recreating) the position for the organization but also crafting fundamentally new approaches to how we did our work. The organizing and advocacy work we did with youth, for example, became a model shared across the country. In fact, after the first 3 years or so when I was first developing the work, I rarely did the same thing year over year. The work was evolving so quickly and the organization gave me so much flexibility that the model moved from innovative, but isolated, programming to a national best-practice in a couple of years. With that, I transitioned to helping other organizations and cities improve their work with youth, and even for that one special week helping train the Trinidad and Tobago Ministries of Education and Local Government.

Just as a reminder, my training for all of this work at the time amounted to a Cranbrook MFA and my life up to that point. Business school came next.

As the work evolved, I realized that there were limits of what would get funded in the traditional nonprofit sector, particularly as I pushed its boundaries, and I began exploring other business models. In fact, my first couple of years of consulting were developed as a revenue generator for Oasis Center, which was a nonprofit. We were exploring new financial sustainability options for a traditional social services agency.

So, when I went to business school, I was looking for new models, new language, and new strategies. I was looking for new angles and approaches that I could take and make my own.

In fact, here is the essay I submitted in my application:

Candidly, I am not much of a planner. This, however, should not be misinterpreted in any way as my lacking direction or vision. My life is about learning and learning for the sake of meaningful and transformative action. I seek and choose opportunities that help me cross cultural, practical, and intellectual boundaries for the purpose of improving social and community conditions.

By its very nature, such systemic work cannot and will not be done in silos. So, as I set goals and plan my personal and professional life, I aspire to be deeply present in every moment across diverse settings with a broad awareness, a critical mind, and with a variety of languages (nonprofit, business, social justice, etc.). The ability to cross these critical divides, to operate in a "space between," and to translate the seemingly disparate languages across community sectors will be the skill that allows me to transform community conditions, to transform systems, and to capitalize and build upon common interest in lieu of emphasizing supposedly insurmountable differences.

Movement toward this sort of cross-system connecting can be seen with varied results between business and nonprofits. The business community is investing in new models as it celebrates social entrepreneurship and develops schools targeted at such strategies. Its "double" and "triple bottom line" language and concepts of "blended value" further wrap typically social sector philosophies around business models.

Similarly, nonprofits have begun looking and acting more like businesses – seeking earned-income strategies, talking about efficiency and impact differently, and even considering "client" needs and desires more in the development of products and services. And yet, for a variety of reasons, not the least of which is the lack of financial and educational infrastructure, the nonprofit community shows relatively few signs of the commitment to or success of the blended models of the business community. Nonprofits need new strategies.

I have a life, a family, and a professional career built around youth, communities, and social justice in Nashville. I have an undergraduate education founded in literature and the visual arts. I have a Masters degree in Fine Arts that has nothing to do with creating art and everything to do with living a creative life and generating the life I want to live. In my work, from a youth-focused, nonprofit base, I have generated opportunities and relationships ranging from local neighborhood groups to the Ford Motor Company Fund, from the Nashville Mayor's Office to the Ministry of Education of Trinidad and Tobago, from local schools and nonprofits to the nation's largest coalition for children and youth the America's Promise Alliance.

An MBA will expand my creativity with the tools of entrepreneurship and a sense of business acumen. It will inculcate my social systems thinking with financial and economic systems thinking. It will broaden my language of social change such that I may appeal for change and to change leadership not merely through an altruistic or social lens but through market-based, economic strategy.

Basically, long before I had conceived of writing this book, I had set it up with this brief essay! Who knew!?

But, after a year and a half of classes in macro and micro economics, finance, corporate valuation, operations, HR, accounting, statistics, organizational behavior, and so forth, it was in a class called "Launching the Venture" led by Michael Burcham that I finally realized why I was in business school. This is also when the value of my MFA and experience in the visual arts proved real assets to the experience. Things clicked for me.

The class was a business accelerator…accelerated! In just a half dozen classes over two months or so, we were to create and be prepared to launch a business. We had to articulate the business, the product, define the market and the opportunity, the competition, craft strategy, project financials, and so on. It all would culminate in a presentation to a panel of venture capitalists, who may actually invest in our company. Regardless, they would publically critique and rank the teams best to worst. *Publicly rank us best to worst!* It was go time! Every ounce of competitive spirit left in all of us was ignited.

Coincidentally, or maybe not, one of my teammates went to undergrad at Savannah College of Art and Design and was from a family of artists. In fact, prior to coming to business school, he had started his own business creating gessoed art panels using a proprietary family recipe for gesso, passed down for generations since the Renaissance. The business had already been launched but he had had to shut it down for a variety of reasons. As I would soon learn in my own company, there are more ways to fail than succeed! For our "venture", we re-conceived and re-launched his art panels business.

In the second week of class, we had our first presentations. Randomly selected teams got to present their product and their landscape analysis to the rest of the class and, of course, to Burcham. I was thrilled! I was excited and motivated like I had not been for months in the program. It was Cranbrook critique all over again. The energy. The intensity. The learning. The feedback. The competition. The progress. It didn't take long to find the artists in the group.

The first team swaggered confidently to the front to present their work. They proceeded through their deck. I don't remember much about it, to be honest. But, when they finished, Burcham immediately began asking pointed questions, highlighting weaknesses in process, logic, and calling out sloppy work. I am sure he was just making an example of the team, setting the stage for what the class would entail, but Burcham publicly dismantled a good portion of what they had done. And, as the team attempted to defend their logic, or just got personally defensive, the critique only intensified. It got uncomfortable as the team attempted to "save face" among their peers; again, only digging themselves deeper in the critique.

I sat there totally engaged, entertained. I was not happy for anyone's sense of embarrassment at all. It wasn't about that. And, it wasn't about that for Burcham either. It was first and foremost about quality work, and in entrepreneurship, as well as art, getting to quality work takes a huge dose of humility. They don't teach humility in business school. And, it is not exactly a business attribute frequently featured in Forbes or the Wall Street Journal.

But, as Picasso suggested "Every act of creation is first an act of destruction."

I was also excited because it was the first time in a year and a half of business school when I felt I was on home turf. This kind of group critique was what I had already spent two years doing at Cranbrook. I was a bit nostalgic actually! But, what it highlighted for me again is just how relevant the creative process is, and yet, how it so often is sacrificed for the sake of appearances. I was reminded how short-term validation and myopic metrics often trump learning and the creative process.

Cranbrook critiques were brutal. Each person had a minimum of two formal critiques per semester, with numerous others big and small in between. But, your critique day was yours and yours only. The class gathered in the gallery and observed and discussed whatever artwork you put in front of them. Some people were vicious. Some people were useless. But, most provided constructive feedback that helped you improve and propelled your work forward. The job of the department head was to keep it productive, or push it to its most destructive, if that is what the work and the artist really needed.

I remember at one of my critiques one of may studio mates questioning why I had signed a group of prints I had made that happened to be adapted from other images. She was very confused about my claim to authorship, and was insistent, not that I answer why I had done so, but that I agree with her that I had made some sort of calamitous mistake in doing so.

In another critique, a studio mate had created an installation, beautiful in its execution, but according to her about her "fear of ovals." I have no idea what we ended up talking about at that one. I just remember a lot of awkward silence. In fact, that was just the critique required for the situation. The silence was deafening and told the whole story.

In others, grown adults cried, stormed out of the room, yelled, and developed friends and enemies that I suspect to some degree persist to this day. It was amazing and horrifying and transformative, if, and only if, you could see the process for what it was and not get caught up in surface drama and pettiness. It was a huge opportunity, all of Cranbrook was. Those were two of the most miserable years I have ever spent, and probably the two most transformative of my life.

Over 150 artists were with me at Cranbrook, and it was pretty obvious at our thesis show who had been open to critique and who had instead been defensive, who was there to be creative and who was their to have their creativity validated. The work of the former had transformed and deepened and in many cases, like my own, gone in totally new directions. For the latter, their work literally looked the exact same as it did when they first started. They had spent two years and a lot of defensive energy, not to mention tens of thousands of dollars, to leave Cranbrook just how they entered it.

Their own sense of themselves as artists, almost as a finite concept, was fueled by a systematic confirmation bias. So, as they put their work up and sat through their own brutal critiques, the only thing they heard, accepted, or respected were insights that ultimately confirmed their work, their interpretations, and their direction. If your feedback did otherwise, you just didn't understand. And, this isn't just a Cranbrook thing. It's endemic in the art world. Look around at the artists in your community or even the artists in the books and magazines and see who is continuing to create and who is making the same stuff over and over again. To make matters worse, market driven creativity begs artists, to some degree, to keep creating the stuff "people like" or that sells. But, that discussion is for a different book altogether.

Steve Jobs summed it up: "If you don't cannibalize yourself, someone else will."

At its essence as a process, as Jobs also knew well, creativity requires prototyping, whether we are talking about our own growth or the production of a piece of art or new technology we are putting out to the world. But, prototyping is deceptively complex, not necessarily in the process of making and iterating, but particularly in the presence required to do it well.

"Effective prototyping requires the capacity to stay connected and grounded in your deepest source of inspiration and larger will while simultaneously learning to listen to all of the feedback your actions elicit. If you're open, the larger environment will continuously tell you what you need to learn. The feedback you get from experiments will give helpful clues about how to shape, mold, and concretize what is beginning to form – but only if you learn to listen and set aside your negative reactions to "not getting it right" from the outset. This is a secret that highly creative people know tacitly."[20]

It's not about being right, or getting it right, concepts that both produce creative paralysis.

It's about being open to the tension between your "source" and the feedback received when you attempt to share that with the world. The source is not inherently "right" and neither is the feedback.

This proved as true in entrepreneurship as it did at Cranbrook. As I mentioned previously, after 10 years in nonprofit work, I decided to make the jump to co-found Zeumo, which started as a platform to help increase student engagement through more effective communication in schools and community-based organizations. It was a natural extension of all of the work I had done to date. It just happened to be for profit and I just happened to know absolutely nothing about technology. So, I knew I had a new learning curve, but that I brought a lot of useful knowledge and experience to the work.

---

[20] Senge, Peter M. *Presence: Exploring Profound Change in People, Organizations, and Society*. New York: Doubleday, 2005. 148. Print.

We beta tested the product in 4 high schools and got completely crushed. Our product was beta. It wasn't ready for use by teenagers who don't care about school, don't like their classes, and as research shows, despite being technophiles, don't like anything about anything when it comes to technology. Or, they like it for 15 minutes and then move on. I won't start on the disgruntled teachers who missed the opportunity to talk about how students can be creative, provide meaningful feedback to our team who had invited their collaboration, and so forth. They missed a chance not to use our product but to show their students how to take risks. Alternately, I should acknowledge those teachers and principals who not only tried our product but also encouraged their students to engage with us and provide us feedback. These teachers understood learning and demonstrated their own creativity. As a result, their students got to see what it was like to try and start your own business. If you want to read about how education kills creativity, I recommend Ken Robinson's work. Yes, it's depressing, but his insights on how we might create better schools for students are invaluable.

Anyway, as a result of this most brutal experience, I am now advocating that beta testing technology with young people and teachers in schools be added to the list of practices deemed torture by the federal government. No one should experience that.

But, we had a lot of feedback to filter through. A bit was useful, a lot really wasn't. We kept working, kept building, and ultimately re-launched with a pilot in 16 schools.

Feedback grew by an order of magnitude. Again, some useful; most not so much.

Receiving feedback and translating it into creative, productive insight is complicated. We have to listen for understanding when people share their ideas or complaints. Feedback comes loaded with all sorts of biases and different perspectives, some of which are relevant some of which not at all. We received a ton of feedback based on misunderstandings about what the product was, was supposed to do, etc. We had teachers show up at a training one time in workout clothes expecting a Zumba class. No shit. And, to make it even better, when they found out what the training was actually for, they left!

We received feedback based on people's disdain for other technologies they already had to use. Their students hated them. They hated them. Even so, we heard about how our product should be more like email, or classroom management tools, or wikis, or teacher websites, or… You get the point. If we listened to feedback and took it at face value, we would have built a product that looked just like all the products out there that most teachers don't like and students were already not using!

I read a blog around this time that I immediately quoted and put up on my desk (unfortunately I didn't source it and now can't find it!). The authors said: "we listened to the people and not the problem and complicated the hell out of both of our products."

That's the reality and challenge of a startup trying to get to market. It's also that challenge of the artist who opens himself to critique. We have a vision of what the product could be and perhaps will be once we get a little revenue flowing and a chance to iterate on it. Differently than the artist, however, as an entrepreneur we don't get revenue flowing unless our early users are happy with the product! There's a tighter relationship there with the audience, and a tighter relationship with your startup team trying to make it happen.

Peter Thiel defines a startup as "the largest group of people you can convince of a plan to build a different future."[21]

If we have any chance of building that future, we can't just make a pile of features that people asked for. We have to be a solution; even if it's for a problem they may have trouble articulating. We have to listen for understanding as our client articulates his needs, but also to see the opportunity and the solution with a depth the client may not have. This requires delicate communication and actually delivering the right technology. Like the quantum relationship, our solution helps clarify the problem just as much as the problem helps direct our product. They exist in dynamic relation to each other. So, again, even in entrepreneurship, a

---

[21] Thiel, Peter A., and Blake Masters. *Zero to One: Notes on Startups, or How to Build the Future*. Crown Business, 2014. 10. Print.

problem-centered approach won't suffice to create a different future.

Destroy Something You Made

Sometimes our "finished" work can actually be what prevents us from becoming. We get stuck. We stop listening. We stop learning. As artists, we often believe our work is inherently precious and valuable and meaningful because...well... it is to us. Well, it's not. And, thinking so is a trap and counter to the idea of the creative process.

The most important lesson I learned as a developing artist was accidental, and if I hadn't been forced into it, I would have almost certainly continued to hang on to my every "masterpiece."

I had never built anything. Anything. I had never worked in a woodshop. I don't measure things particularly well and don't pay that much attention to detail. So, building things was not exactly in my creative wheelhouse. So, of course, when I decided to build something in my first sculpture class, I went big. I built a large cube that looked like a kid's A-B-C block, but you could easily get inside. I'll spare you the details of my early efforts at conceptual art, but the piece did make it into the student show! People got inside. People liked it.

Enter ego: Yes, I am Artist. Brilliance. Can you feel that!?

I went home for the summer while the Student Show wrapped up and when I came back, there was my masterpiece, sitting in the hallway. As I stood looking at it, one of my teachers approached and said: "You have to get that out of here."

Apparently, everyone didn't feel it should be a permanent installation in the studio hallways. And, apparently, it didn't fit through any doorways I could reasonably get to. Hmm…what to do!?

The answer was back in the sculpture studio, where it all began… and it was a "saws-all". After the initial horror of the thought of destroying my piece, I plugged in the saw and gingerly started to cut. Within moments, I must have looked like the artist version of the Texas Chainsaw Massacre. I ripped that thing to pieces…sawing…splintering…crashing…cutting…and almost certainly bleeding.

And, in the final act of destruction, I dragged my masterpiece piece-by-piece outside and slung it over the side of the dumpster. Holy crap that felt good. It was humbling…and then completely liberating!

I have created art more freely since that day. And, when I teach art, I actually require my students to destroy a piece. I want them to become artists, not just to make pieces of art.

Fast forward fifteen years or so, and I was helping start Zeumo. (It's not lost on me, by the way, that the first sculpture I built and destroyed was also about improving education.) While we were still struggling to get distribution in a number of large school districts, we were presented with a new opportunity: "We need this kind of app in hospitals."

We were failing slowly in education and had to be humble enough to acknowledge it. We also had to have the courage to try something else, to keep iterating. Long story short, we seized the opportunity and, having invested countless hours and hundreds of thousands of dollars with a vision for helping high school students, we took the proverbial saws-all to the education app.

Humility is not about accepting loss or defeat. Humility is about owning the process of exploration and finding the strength and energy to keep doing it. It's about putting failure in its proper place in our art and in our lives – right at the heart of what we are creating.

The reality is that most of our ideas suck. If they don't, we aren't generating enough ideas. And, if you don't believe it, then you don't really want to be all that creative. Bad ideas don't make you a bad person, a bad artist, or any less creative. They are a requirement. Any artist or entrepreneur or other creator with a few scars and a dose of humility realizes this.

My friend, designer, sculptor, quilter, and philosopher, Thomas Knauer, author of Modern Quilt Perspectives: 12 Patterns for Meaningful Quilts eloquently and summarily described the creator's reality to me one day: "Most of what you make is the utter shite that helps you figure out how to stop perpetually making utter shite so stop worrying so much about the fact that you make utter shite and get on with the process of figuring out how to make less utter shite and perhaps actually make something that is merely shite or even one day, if you are very lucky, something that isn't shite at all."

I am embarrassed when I look back at my old notebooks full of skill-less sketches, weak philosophizing, trite designs, and poorly conceived pseudo-conceptual artworks. Good lord, I hope when I am dead and gone no one ever shares them on Antiques Roadshow. Any respect I may have earned in making people think I am creative or smart or a reasonable artist will certainly be obliterated. Like me, most artists use the notebook to get the noise out of our heads. Most artists don't have Leonardo Di Vinci's notebooks. (Although, I suspect he had a lot of "shite" in there too, but history just doesn't talk about those parts!)

Again, shite is OK. It's even good. It happens.

And, while I started off saying that most of our ideas suck, I should probably step back and reframe this a bit more positively: some of our ideas don't suck. (Isn't that much nicer!?)

In that sense, it is still imperative to fill that notebook with ideas! It's the only way you make room for new ones, and, more importantly, decide which ones are worth iterating on. And, deciding which ideas to iterate on and how is the key to the creative process, whether in art, business, or life.

You create on the energy and process of iteration, not the fact of that initial idea. You create by becoming.

PART II:
SEEING

"From a very early age, we are taught to break apart problems, to fragment the world. This apparently makes complex tasks and subjects more manageable, but we pay a hidden, enormous price. We can no longer see the consequences of our actions; we lose our intrinsic connection to a larger world." - Peter Senge[22]

People and Places

That morning just like almost every other Saturday morning of my childhood, I rolled out of bed and stumbled crusty-eyed to the television. The house was silent, parents exhausted – raising three children – sister staying at a friend's house- and a brother entering puberty, wanting little more in life than a solid 12 hours of sleep and 12 hours of shooting basketball to complete his existence. I kept the TV volume low- caught somewhere between a fear of waking my brother and dying to have him sitting there next to me. I probably watched a couple of cartoons - Tom and Jerry to be certain – some classic episodes of The Three Stooges - and maybe even an episode of Saved by the Bell.

During a commercial break, all of which were essentially the same, telling me all about the new GI Joe aircraft carrier, 6 feet long, with all kinds of moving parts, the new He-Man Castle Grey Skull with working moat draw bridge and the new Cabbage Patch Kids doll that was OK for boys to play with, I went downstairs (the

---

[22] Senge, Peter M. *The Fifth Discipline: The Art and Practice of the Learning Organization.* New York: Doubleday/Currency, 1990. 3. Print.

creaking steps calculatedly waking my parents) and got a bowl of Lucky Charms – "so magically delicious!"

As I hit the bottom step to head back upstairs, face down in my bowl trying to see if I could inhale a marshmallow and sloshing a bit of sugary milk on the carpet, Mom greeted me from behind the wall with a cheery but tired "Good morning." I half whispered back my good morning to make sure she knew I was being as quiet as I possibly could and all of that banging around in the kitchen was in no way meant to wake her, which of course it was. Dad kept snoring.

I went upstairs to eat my Lucky Charms while watching the commercials for Cocoa Crisp and Rice Crispies, convinced that I would be much happier if I had a bowl of either of them. I continued my charade of quietness by turning up the TV and clanking my cereal bowl down on the glass coffee table. My brother's current growth spurt had rendered all of my noise-making completely ineffective.

Two hours later, my spoonful of sugar milk beginning to dry out on the coffee table, my patience for my brother wholly exhausted, the hours of Saturday morning children's programming beginning to bore me, I headed back downstairs and sat down next to my Mom enjoying her morning coffee and reading the paper in the kitchen.

My life growing up was pretty normal, except for that it wasn't at all.

In the mid 1970s my parents, then with two young children and pregnant with me, decided they didn't want to raise their kids in the homogenous (read all-white) suburbs. And, for some reason, they thought it a good idea to move into a house two doors down from where my father was helping investigate a murder. My Mom told me that Maw (her Mom) cried and cried about our moving to such a terrible part of town. I can just imagine that conversation!

The house cost $9,000, but the banks had redlined the neighborhood so you couldn't get a loan for more than $5000 to support any renovations. There was a hole in the floor in the dining room, the one room that was actually lived in, that the sole resident had cut to let the water from the leaky roof drain out. There were no sidewalks. There were no stop signs. And, we had a phone booth in the front yard primarily managed by pimps and prostitutes.

Just a short time into their renovations, my parents saw a young, local reporter named Oprah Winfrey and a camera crew in the park across the street apparently reporting on something for the local news station. Excited and hoping to hear a story about the revitalization starting to happen in this part of the city, they tuned in that night to hear something like this:

"Oprah Winfrey reporting: I am standing here today on the most dangerous street in the city of Nashville. Home to crimes ranging from car theft to drug deals, from simple burglary to cold-blooded murder. Today is no different. At approximately 1 PM in broad daylight, a man was shot to death just down the street from where I am standing. Witnesses say that two men, a middle aged, white man with tattoos on each forearm, a large scar on his cheek and a young black male wearing a black trench and coat and black stocking cap began fighting. The young black man pulled a gun and shot the other three times in the chest. The confrontation appears to have been drug related. Police are looking for a black male, age 25-35, last seen wearing a black trench coat and running south on eighth toward the James Cayce Homes."

Ahh, the same stories we would hear for the next 20 years. At one point, we had to change our route coming home from school because of several murders that had happened along it. We could not drive down the street a block from our home because there were crack houses, prostitution, dangerous vacant lots, and people hanging out in the streets.

At one point during their long process of renovation, for which my Dad actually stopped working (and he provided the primary family income which meant we were also broke), my parents returned to the house after several weeks away to find an extension cord running from our house to the neighbors where it was fueling the window unit air conditioning of a 7 apartment slum, with all the windows open, in 90 degree weather.

Residents of these 7 apartments included a Pentecostal preacher and just across the hall a prostitute.

The man in the house across the street would climb up to his third floor attic window and howl like a wolf at anyone walking down the street.

The nursing home a block behind us was closed, but was full of homeless people, and particularly junkies.

Theirs were the needles and bottles I avoided when mowing my yard.

Boots lived in the house on the other side of the alley and spent much of his time walking around the neighborhood.

"Hey Boots!" I shouted as I always did despite never receiving a response.

It was OK. Boots was busy. He walked the street with the focus of a CEO working on a deal. Hammering out details, arguing his point, determined to be heard. His worn khaki left pant leg rolled to the knee, once explained to my Mom as being in preparation for a flood, his Tom Landry-style hat perched carefully on his head, and a worn, white button-up recalling a day when Boots was not so thin and frail. I really don't ever recall laughing or making fun, I just somehow understood that yeah, Boots is talking to his elbow, his left elbow specifically.

He walked in short but determined steps, his heavy black shoes perhaps explaining the nickname and offering a timeline for just how long Boots had been walking the streets and talking to his elbow. His skin camouflaged in the muddled and muted tones of his now off-white shirt and his faded pants. His pulled-up black sock describing the shape of a left leg that was otherwise almost transparent. His face thin and gaunt with wrinkles tight and sharp was more a story of the shadow of his hat than a determining genetic tale.

I knew him by his clothes and his posture in the setting of the sidewalk across the street from my house. I don't know much more.

If Boots is the earliest "street friend" that I remember, Walter and Flavio are two of the best. Walter and Flavio were drinking buds. Walter was an illiterate WWII veteran who brought his mail to our house for my parents to help him read. I have no idea where his mail was delivered. Flavio was the friendliest, floppiest, drunk you have ever met, and his speech flowed fluidly between Spanish and English.

One Fourth of July, I was shooting fireworks in the park across the street. (The Fourth of July and New Years were always an interesting time as it became a favorite past-time of mine during these seasons to challenge myself to decipher gun fire from M-80's.) I was shooting bottle rockets that day with a friend from school, one of the few whose parents actually would allow him to spend the night in our neighborhood, and I heard the familiar jingle of Walter's shopping cart coming up the street. Walter strolled up, his cigarette appeared more stuck in a wrinkle in his face than in his mouth, and parked the cart on the edge of the street.

I wondered if Walter had just grabbed any old cart or if he had done some shopping around. His was one of the shiniest carts that I had seen, no rust, few dents, no remnant cola spills. It did, however, have the textbook front wheel that never touched the ground. It just hovered there, revolving seemingly of its own initiative, never a part of the rest of the cart.

As Walter approached alone, I noticed that Flavio was already passed out cold, sitting up on the wall on the opposite corner from our house. His head sagged like a medicine ball as if his body had just collapsed under its weight. I think if he had been left there long enough, the softness of his broken down leathery skin, the boneless mass of his body would have ultimately melted together leaving some sort of amorphous spillage. But that's why Walter was there. I think it was his unspoken goal to keep Flavio from dissolving.

"Hey!" Walter squeezed out in a gruff whisper. "Hey, Anderson. Let me see one of those."

"Sir?"

"Let me see one of those rockets."

"Oh. Ok. Here you go."

Walter took a bottle rocket from me and walked slowly over to the chain link fence that defined the boundaries of the park's softball field. He carefully propped the rocket in its web. By the time he got over there, Walter was so tickled at himself that he could hardly set the rocket straight. I looked at my friend to see if he was all right and he just looked confused. Watching Walter that day was like watching a kid my age who was up to no good and was having a blast at it. He was just one of us.

It took a second, but I soon understood what he was up to. Walter was aiming the rocket at Flavio. He turned to me and winked, grinning a charming toothless half-smile as he held on to his cigarette in the other half. He took the cigarette from his mouth and lit the bottle rocket.

It ignited and took off. Fortunately for Flavio, it took one of those unpredictable curves and exploded a good 20 feet from him. Walter tried again. The next one took off and exploded right next to Flavio, about five feet to his left. Walter was growing increasingly tickled, I was laughing but also worried about Flavio, and my friend was still silent and dumbfounded. Third time's a charm. Walter lit the third rocket and it shot and exploded right between Flavio's dangled legs, right between the wickets.

Flavio didn't budge. He remained there with his head bending the trunk of his spine like a ripe fruit unwilling to drop. A body had never looked so heavy while actually remaining upright. It was a delicate balance of physics I couldn't figure out. To this day, I am not sure that anyone can really be that drunk. I wonder sometimes if Flavio wasn't just having his own good time with Walter by not letting him win.

There were still other neighbors like Lash who are part of the fabric of my upbringing but who I only knew as part of that fabric. I only knew as a child looking, seeing.

Lash lived on the block behind us. I have no idea if he went by Lash, if my parents just called him Lash or what, but he was as dependable as the morning sun. For the virgin ears, the crack of Lash's bullwhip muddied the other neighborhood percussion: bass, backfiring cars, fireworks and gunfire. But to me, it simply said, "it's a beautiful day." Lash and his bullwhip told you the weather before you could even step outside. If you heard it, the weather must be clear and warm. He stayed wrapped safely behind a chain link fence, never veering more than a half step away from presumably where his parents or caretakers (I never saw them) had planted him early that morning. Or perhaps he planted himself. I don't know. I never saw him come or go. He was just either there or not. I also never saw anyone else who lived there with him.

Lash had some sort of significant intellectual disability, and I would guess was in his twenties, thirties, forties, who knows. His body showed the signs of someone whose physical and mental limitations had created a structure that was sizable but only temporary. He stood in the yard with his dirtied blue-gray button-up shirt and gray Dickies, softened to the point of pajamas. Lash stood alone with his shoulders slung way back as a counterbalance to a bulging stomach. His black shoes, with only the soles and toes peaking out, appeared to be a good size-and-a-half too large, strings torqued and tied in a strangle hold hoping to maintain their hold on his feet. He stood in the front yard of his house and bull whipped the old hackberry roots bubbling from the ground. No one knew why. At least no one I knew knew why.

In the unknown of his world, the crack of the bullwhip must have been empowering. The energy generated from that raw leather strip, formed in his hand, Lash's story, his word to the world. Action and reaction. Power. Production. It gave him an edginess, a danger, a virility. The sound of that bullwhip creating a sparkling explosion of color, of adrenaline. The vibration shooting through his body like an electrical shock. He felt every crack that we only heard. It must have been beautiful; he had been doing it for years.

Strangely, I haven't seen Lash for decades and I still live in the same house. In fact, I haven't seen anyone come in or out of that house for decades, and other than Lash 25 years ago, maybe ever! And yet, as I was writing this, a new neighbor who lives next door actually told me Lash still lives there with his family! His name is Billy. I am glad to at least know that now, but dumbfounded by the fact the he still lives there, that anyone lives there. Life is strange.

But, my neighbors like Billy weren't always just eccentric or mentally challenged. There was a darker side in both perception and reality. The year I was born and the year after my parents bought their house, the Nashville Banner, one of the city's leading newspapers, wrote the following about our neighborhood of Edgefield: "Out of the gutters, all you winos. Back in your raincoats, you perverts. Edgefield is going respectable." Nice.

This was my community. These were my neighbors. Some were my friends. Others scared the shit out of me. And, there was no distance from which to stand and just look at them, much less judge them. I had to see them, I was taught to see them, by very diligent and patient parents. I had to see them for who they were to me and my family and my community, not as generic concepts of the poor, the vagrant, or as derelicts or statistics.

I am not trying to romanticize any of this or the brutal example of life that many of these people represented. It was tragic in many ways. The point is that as the white, middle-class, Christian-raised, heterosexual, mentally stable, educated male that I am, I was the odd ball. If you couldn't see that, you weren't looking.

I would come to understand years later after my Dad's struggles with Depression and ultimate suicide that he, in fact, was more akin to our neighbors than I understood as a child. His empathy with their lives, pain, and circumstances was real, and reveals a lot about him and his own struggles. More about that later.

So, I guess it's perhaps not shocking that a kid cultivated in this environment would grow up thinking and seeing the world a little differently. So, it's also probably not a shock that I would find my way to the world of visual art, or it would find its way to me.

It's worth noting here that my honors thesis show in undergrad was a series of paintings and prints depicting faces and bodies of my "street" neighbors, two of whom, Delmas and Luanne, were also very dear friends. I worked for months and months on this show. I worked from photos my Mom had taken for me on my street and in the park across the street. I transformed the gallery space. I brought in park benches from around campus. I opened the view so you could still see the campus outside while viewing the work inside. I hung the paintings and prints such that with a turn of the head the viewer moved from face to body to face of otherwise nameless, unidentifiable, and presumably homeless, figures. From intimate to nondescript, from human to object, and back again.

Here is how I explained my motivation in my artist's statement, the first I had ever written, for the show:

"Growing up in downtown Nashville, I found myself exposed to a part of life that most of my suburban friends and classmates did not know existed. My neighborhood rests as an island of middle-class living in a sea of subsidized living, government housing and even homelessness. It seemed that every time I walked about of my house I was greeted by a new face: either walking to work, looking for work, walking to the soup kitchen or walking to the community center... In my years of college, however, I have been separated from the city environment and I have found that I greatly miss it... (But) what have I done with my unique gift of being exposed to a world so different from my own? Very little, it seems. This body of work is an attempt for me to grow closer to and become more aware of these people who have meant so much to my life but whom I have also taken for granted."

I am still challenged by this reflection today, even as I am back home and actually living and raising my daughters in the same house – albeit a considerably more gentrified community. I am still trying to see the people and the places that have so influenced who and what I continue to become.

The Whole

"Contrary to our strong sense that we usually know what's going on around us, people don't perceive the world as it actually is. Never mind that our senses are designed to register only certain kinds of stimuli – certain wavelengths of light or frequencies of sound, for example – and that everything that lies outside our sense modalities goes undetected. Even in the realm of the knowable, our experience of the events that unfold around us is accompanied by an ongoing internal commentary about them that modifies the nature of our experience. In everyday language, we "talk to ourselves" about what we experience. Furthermore, what we say to ourselves about what's happening is often not correct." – Mark Leary[23]

"The physical eye assesses and establishes the rudiments of compositional structure…Then, the eye of the mind (soul) intercedes, penetrates, and prevails in places uninhabitable by the physical eye alone." - A Guide to Drawing[24]

I always knew I loved art. I loved to create. But, once I got into studio courses in college, I realized that art was not something I liked to do: it is who I am. I love the feedback. I love the challenge, the smell, the process, the thrill, the godliness of bringing something new to the world.

---

[23] Leary, Mark R. *The Curse of the Self Self-awareness, Egotism, and the Quality of Human Life*. Oxford: Oxford UP, 2004. 54 Print.
[24] Mendelowitz, Daniel Marcus, David Faber, and Duane Wakeham. *A Guide to Drawing*. 6th ed. New York: Holt, Rinehart & Winston, 2003.50. Print.

But, art also began to create me, that defining quantum reality of one existing only in relationship the other, when I learned how to see. It happened in a carefully constructed a-ha moment, one that changed me forever.

I was sitting with about eight other developing artists in a studio at L'Ecole Marchutz just outside of Aix-en-Provence, France. All of the swinging door windows and shutters wrapping the cool terra cotta tiled studio were flung open to let the famous Provencal light fill the studio. We rarely used anything but natural light.

One day, my studio mates and I were gathered around our teacher Alan Roberts who was holding an image of a still life. I don't really recall what was in the still life, but I do remember being struck by how "realistic" it seemed. It was beautifully painted, and was considered art-historically a "significant" work. We discussed the piece. Critiqued it. Talked about color and light and composition and so forth.

Then he pulled out a Cezanne still life, some fruit on a table with a ceramic bowl, maybe a pitcher. It was comparatively raw. The line was loose. The canvas shown through – was it even complete? The color and painting style were classic Cezanne and the composition compelling.

So, with both still lifes in front of us, Alan started talking about seeing and painting "the whole." He talked about our relationship as artists with our subject and the ways the various elements of nature, even organized in a still life, relate to each other. An apple relates to an orange relates to the negative space and shadow relate to the ceramic bowl. None exists as an independent object, but all as a whole.

Then, he did something strange: he turned both masterpieces upside down. We sat. Looking. Quietly. Finally, he asked us to talk about the two pieces again, as they were now presented.

I don't know if everyone saw it, but my world had just changed - forever. Masterpiece #1, not the Cezanne, that was so compelling and beautiful, completely fell apart when it was upside down. I could almost hear the clashing and clanging as the individual elements of the still life seemed to fall off the canvas. One piece fell of the bottom right of the canvas, another to the left, another seemingly suspended in air with no relation to anything. Upside down, our minds stopped filling in the blanks and making connections that weren't really there. The Cezanne painting, on the other hand, still looked fine, less recognizable as specific objects since they were upside down, but nothing was falling apart.

Cezanne had seen the objects, not just looked at them, and had painted the whole. Debashis Chatterjee distinguishes Cezanne's way of seeing from the way the artist of the other still life saw and most of the rest of us see: "We are visual ragpickers. In the ordinary state of consciousness, we passively pick up fragmented visual impressions of objects or events. This is a low-energy activity like mechanical picking up of bits and pieces from our environment. High-energy seeing involves not accumulating objects or events but seeing something more. It involves the discipline of seeing through events to the invisible processes that shape those events...True seeing is not just glancing the visible surface of objective reality. True seeing involves perceptive vision of the invisible potential of objective reality."[25]

Cezanne understood and had the discipline to perceive that the objects in a still life and their interactions with each other are, in fact, visual and relational events, not mere static objects. And, this is what he painted. This is why they held together even upside down.

In this moment, sitting in that studio in Aix, I began not just to see art differently, but to see my relationships, my challenges and opportunities, the world differently. A discipline of trying to see the relationships between things, the whole has guided my life and work since that exact moment (which is not to say I have always been successful at it!).

I later learned that the business version of such seeing is called systems thinking. But, I also quickly learned that it was more of a concept – an ideal - than a reality for most systems and most leaders. Whether working with a school system, a political system, or an organizational system, I found few people conceiving of the whole, much less leading it. We all tend to focus on our part, our job, our task. This myopia is both the symptom and source of the classic CYA (cover your ass) syndrome in organizations. It's the reason "systems" too

---

[25] Chatterjee, Debashis. *Leading Consciously a Pilgrimage toward Self-mastery*. Boston, Mass.: Butterworth-Heinemann, 1998. 2. Print.

often end up as mere collections of silos. Individual work becomes the job. People assume if they do their job the work will get done – or, worst case, don't care beyond their job anyway. The goal becomes task completion and personal satisfaction (or at least good evaluations) rather than creativity and engagement for the betterment of the whole. No one holds a vision. No one is driven by shared organizational values. The whole is merely the sum of its parts (never mind where and how those parts overlap, contradict, or otherwise waste potentially shared resources).

Famous for his leadership of Hermann Miller, Max De Pree describes it like this: "Parts are often mistaken for wholes. Ideas viewed as complete when they are incomplete. Relationships considered well formed when they are insufficiently formed. Values are taken for final statements when, in fact, they are only beginnings. Were these parts recognized for what they are, and were we to work toward their completion – were we to keep "becoming" as individuals – we would be better off as persons, as corporations, and as institutions."[26]

If we remain a process, keep becoming, and see and acknowledge the whole of the moving parts making up that process, we will be more dynamic individuals and create more sustainable organizations and systems. If we design organizations and systems, on the other hand, that allow, or worse, force our ideas of who we are as individuals to stagnate or to fragment, if we just start managing systems and organizations as fact, we again

---

[26] Pree, Max. *Leadership Is an Art*. New York: Doubleday, 2004. 144. Print.

"slaughter our finest impulses." We end up with lives we never wanted to lead. We build organizations that don't deliver what we intended. And, we build social and cultural systems that we in turn play victim to.

The reality is that every organization or system is perfectly designed to deliver the outcomes it delivers – and, just another reminder: we created them.

If you think on that for just a moment, it's both painfully obvious and painfully…well…painful. But, for anyone working to change the outcomes that are important to them in education, business, politics, social justice, or otherwise, this simple reality tells us where our efforts must be directed: at the systems that we have, advertently or inadvertently, designed to underperform (or to perform exceptionally toward outcomes we never intended).

Under this premise, the school system that is struggling with dropouts is perfectly designed to generate those dropouts.

The justice system that incarcerates men of color at dramatically higher rates than anyone else is perfectly designed to incarcerate men of color.

The political system that generates corruption, gridlock, and weak candidates is perfectly designed to do just that.

System performance is not the sum of its individual elements. It is the interrelated (systemic) performance of its parts. The whole. Systems get misaligned because we build and invest (or disinvest) in them element by element often over long periods of time, and amidst shifting values and visions. And, the more we address individual elements in isolation the more likely we are to create silos and systemic dissonance (the type of boiling-frog dissonance that unfolds over time such that we actually grow to accept it).

Within an organizational system, for example, perhaps we have rewritten our values statement, but our organizational structure is out-of-date or even arbitrary. We revisit our investments (budget, people, etc.), but align them with our organizational structure rather than our strategy (this is my new definition of bureaucracy, by the way). We clarify and document our desired outcomes, but we maintain old strategies that have lost relevance in a changing environment. We improve our product or service delivery, but never invest in our human capital pipeline to support and sustain it.

When we see systemic failure, we cannot blame the system without owning our role in it. We cannot claim that our part of the system is working, and it's everyone else's that's broken. We cannot do fragmented and narrow work and believe it will add up to a healthy whole. It won't.

If we are going to create the system that is perfectly designed to deliver the outcomes we actually want, we need to design, invest, work, and lead systemically. We have to see the whole and have the courage to work with it. Otherwise, we will create systems that are ultimately doomed to fail: paintings that will fall apart when turned upside down.

Your Work and Career

"Life isn't about finding yourself. Life is about creating yourself." - George Bernard Shaw

"The best way to predict the future is to create it."
- Peter Drucker

Judge Smails: *Ty, what did you shoot today?*
Ty Webb: *Oh, Judge, I don't keep score.*
Judge Smails: *Then how do you measure yourself with other golfers?*
Ty Webb: *By height.*
- Caddyshack

Systemic thinking, seeing and working with the whole are difficult. That's why everyone who paints isn't Cezanne and few leaders have had the staying power of Max De Pree or Peter Drucker. As a result, in seeking to create our lives and achieve our definition of success, most of us are actually really harsh on ourselves. Let me clarify: those of us who believe we have the power to create are harsh on ourselves. Those who don't carry this belief, on the other hand, often defer their success, this critical judgment, to others. But, I am assuming that anyone reading this book believes you are a creator and are working hard to create your self and your future. You are seeking something, even if, like me, you aren't always exactly sure what it is.

So, in seeking, we have to maintain the discipline of systemic thinking around our own lives, but also give ourselves some grace in the face of its inevitable challenges and uncertainty. If we are working toward systemic change, whether within ourselves, in our relationships, or in the broader world, we are going to fail more times than not. We have to accept that as part of our work, as part of creating. If it were easy, someone would have done it before and could just show us how to recreate it. If everyone wanted change, it would have already happened. To be creators, we must be able to execute on our vision, values, and aspirations and know that everyone doesn't share or understand them.

As a startup, I saw more clearly than ever that there are far more ways to fail than to succeed. That's the system. Could we get the right team? Could we keep it? Could we build the product we envisioned? Could we sell the product? Could we get people to use it? Could we pay next month's rent (not that much to learn from this one unfortunately)? While we had some key yesses, we also had critical nos. So, to survive and thrive creatively, we must embrace failure. We must own it. We must understand it as generative. We must learn from it. Failure with learning isn't failure. It's learning. So, it's creative.

"All of us fail, and – because they are bold and ambitious – creators fail the most frequently and, often, the most dramatically. Only a person who is willing to pick herself up and "try and try again" is likely to forge creative achievements. And even when an achievement has been endorsed by the field, the prototypical creator rarely rests on her laurels; instead, she proceeds along a new, untested path, fully ready to risk failure time and again in return for the opportunity to make another, different, mark."[27]

For most of us, the creative drive is infinite. It's not just about short-term successes – although those certainly help keep us motivated. It may not even be about success at all – at least as others may define it. It is personal. It is core to our identity. It is our work. For some of us, if we are lucky, or if we go out and make it so, it can even be our job. (Work is about who you are and how you manifest that in the world. A job can be part of that or wholly distinct.) Let's be clear: living and working creatively demands tradeoffs. Instead of a clear pathway, we make the road by walking. Instead of linear learning and steady growth, we have peaks and valleys of both. Instead of a career in the traditional sense, we have a map of our own personal and professional journey. But, it's our journey.

This is why I take issue with how the need for work/life balance as it is typically promoted to us.

We all know the concept. Most of us have probably read a book about it, or even sat through some sort of seminar or workshop on the topic (probably called something like "7 Easy Steps to Balance Work and Life") by some guy who has it all figured out. He has a framework. He has a picture. He has 7 easy steps. Maybe he wrote the book.

---

[27] Gardner, Howard. *Five Minds for the Future*. Pbk. ed. Boston, Mass.: Harvard Business, 2008. 83 Print.

But, the paradigm is corrupt for creators, if not for everyone. As presented, work exists on one end of a continuum; life happens on the other. Its premise is that your work and job are inherently distinct, and your goal is to find the balance in between, fulfilling neither. It is fundamentally uncreative.

Here are a few specific issues with the framework:

Issue #1: The work/life duality is zero sum and linear. The nearer I am to work, the further I am from life, and vice versa. One side takes from the other. As such, it promotes identity schizophrenia, anxiety, and even guilt. In other words, the diametrically opposed forces create potentially paralyzing external pressures rather than generative, creative, internal motivation.

Issue #2: Life, in and of itself, is entirely non-linear and is its own "balancing" act of an endless number of variables, one of which is work. Some are controllable. Some are not. Work and life don't have to be distinct, but rather collectively come from, create, and reinforce (or, worst-case, dismantle) our sense of self. The connection between work and life is a controllable variable for people who choose to create both.

Issue#3: Work and life require different energy and different types of investment and skills. One doesn't really take from the other, but they all do come from the same source (the self). So, cultivation of the self (becoming) is the source of balance, if such a concept actually applies.

Who we are and who we are trying to become is complex. It's messy. It's emerging. It's creative. It evolves over time in all kinds of broadly defined work and amid the relational and existential craziness that is often called life. However each is defined, work and life are just different contexts for our becoming. It is about us not about them.

If we are focused on cultivating and creating our best selves, then we will see when our current work becomes a barrier rather than a facilitator of that process. Alternately, we will see when things happening in our relationships, or otherwise in our personal lives, are inhibiting us from becoming who we want or need to become. We then must have the discipline and courage to adjust our course as needed. We must have the creativity to define a new course and live into it.

Work and life are mediums in the art of becoming fully human. Our goal should be finding art in our life, life in our work, and work in our life. And, that starts with seeing our selves as a whole.

Craft Your Own Narrative

To do this, it helps to be able to craft our own narrative, our own story from that whole. We not only have to be able to narrate it to ourselves as we create it and it creates us, but also share it with others. Crafting that narrative is a way of externalizing and objectifying our experiences so that we can relate to them and reflect on them more deeply, critically, and strategically. I should note here, however, that many of us craft narratives about ourselves that are not for these creative purposes. We craft narratives to deflect, defend, and to obfuscate – to prevent reflection and learning. Clearly, this use of a narrative is not what I am talking about here.

Creative narratives that help us locate and see ourselves more holistically and critically can be core to navigating and creating our personal and professional trajectories. With this in mind, I was invited by a former colleague to do a workshop for a group of young adults serving with Americorps Vista as literacy coaches for the state of Tennessee. Most of them were early-to-mid twenties and starting to think about careers, or at least next steps after their service year(s) were complete. I was supposed to help them think about their "career."

Undoubtedly, the group expected me to give practical tips about resume writing, interviewing and that kind of stuff. I suspect I was supposed to talk about what a career might look like for them in the nonprofit sector – how it might build on the fact that they had been literacy coaches. Not surprisingly to my readers at this point, my goal was to defy these sets of expectations, do something more creative, and to help them think bigger, and yet at the same time more personal.

So, I crafted a brief experience to start that process. I began by separating them into small groups and handing each group a half page of information that included a brief job description and a few bullet points about a fictional job candidate's experience. Their charge was to discuss whether or not they would hire the candidate for the given job and prepare to share with the larger group why or why not. I gave them a few minutes to consider and debate, but for most of the teams it really didn't take that long.

Out of 5 teams, I think one of them offered an interview, and that's mostly because these were the kind of generous and open-minded people who end up serving with Americorps. The other teams didn't even offer an interview - and for really good reasons.

So, then, I let them in on the secret: each of the jobs briefly described were jobs that I personally had held. Youth Organizer. Art Instructor. Educational Consultant. Director of Strategic Initiatives. Chief Product Officer. And, the candidate descriptions were also based on me and my experiences and skills. But, I had paired, for example, job descriptions for Chief Product Officer with my skills and experiences related to fine art and teaching. A youth organizer job description was paired with skills related to business and consulting. And so forth. They were intentionally "mismatched". For emphasis, I also added seemingly irrelevant educational experiences I had had. What can you do with an art degree?

The setup was intended to open a conversation about crafting a narrative, your narrative. Specifically, it was about helping people remove their skills and their learning from their specific job context and locate them in their work. It was to help them think about transferable skills and how they could communicate those skills to a future employer, or higher education institution, to help them understand who they were and what they would bring to the opportunity. In other words, I wanted to impress upon them that they couldn't and shouldn't depend on the interviewer to make a conceptual leap or see how their experience might translate. Their narrative was a controllable variable and they had to own it.

Most employers, for example, at first pass will see us through our jobs (context) first and experiences (skills) second. But, for most of us with atypical "career" paths, we need them to see who we are first. We need to show them the whole, or at least provide a glimpse. We need to show them that our creativity is not bound by context or job. That's our story. That's what we want to talk about. So, the onus is on us to create and drive that narrative and be convincing and convicted about telling it.

I, for example, have to be able to tell how being an artist prepared me to be a youth organizer by forcing me to face "the blank canvas" and to think systemically.

I have to be able to show how being a youth organizer prepared me to co-found a statewide college access network by developing my skills to facilitate non-traditional community partnerships, listen to constituents, and build consensus to take action.

I have to be able to talk about how being an educational consultant prepared me to be a Chief

Product Officer because of my experience listening and responding to client needs and crafting creative solutions.

None of it would be obvious to anyone else. I have to craft and tell my narrative, and you will have to do the same.

And, to be clear, our narrative doesn't have to be all about our wildest successes. Where did we make mistakes? What have we learned? Why? How will those experiences translate to our next opportunity? How do they feed our motivation? Inspire our creativity? Not only does this approach provide a more holistic picture of who we are as candidates for work or for school, it shows that we are also humble and reflective. It shows that we aren't just looking for someone to give us an opportunity but are seeking to create and tell our story fully, with them, through them. We aren't looking for a job: we are looking for the next step in our work. We are hungry and have a few scars to prove that being hungry is part of who we are, not a temporary condition.

In fact, if we can effectively locate them, these scars may be the most compelling part of the narrative. As Sarah Lewis says: "Failure is an orphan until we give it a narrative."[28] Alternately, I think for the creative, the explorer, those who don't follow a narrative readily available or recognizable in the social and cultural archetypes, success can also be an orphan without a narrative. For this group of Americorps Vistas, for example, successes in one-on-one work around literacy,

---

[28] Lewis, Sarah Elizabeth. *The Rise: Creativity, the Gift of Failure, and the Search for Mastery.* New York: Simon & Schuster, 2014. 198. Print.

or policy work, or program development could all feel very specific and difficult to qualify as success outside of that context. Unless they choose to stay in this kind of work forever, they have to translate it to something more transferable, more accessible.

To some extent this is a natural part of being an artist: "Artists smartly spend their careers developing compelling stories about their work. They develop their own perspective on what their art is, what dialogue it has with contemporary and historical trends, how it's distinct, how it reveals new insights into complex ideas, and how the viewer feels or should feel as they engage it. This is just as true for top chefs as for top sculptures (sic)...What is the role of stories among the "professional class?...The most successful professionals infuse what could be a boring, sterile story with more details and implications--transforming the story into salesmanship and persuasion. So when even a spreadsheet requires a story, so too does the analyst and her work."[29]

For the creative class, our stories are often not "boring or sterile" but confusing and seemingly unfocused! I'm reminded of the refrain from a Counting Crows song: "Honey, I'm just trying to make some sense out of me."

We make sense by articulating the active connections among parts of our story. I watched a video online[30] recently of Matt Stone and Trey Parker, the creators of South Park, describing how, as they storyboard an episode, they know they are dead if the concepts and

---

[29] "Why You Should Treat Your Career Like Art" https://www.linkedin.com/pulse/all-art-storytelling-so-your-career-will-gossin-wilson
[30] http://www.theafw.com/blog/south-park-writers-share-their-writing-rule-1/#.

scenes get connected with "and then." That's the boring sterile approach, the describing of the facts. Instead, the elements of their stories, and I suggest yours or mine, should connect with conjunctions like "therefore" and "but" and "because" that, in and of themselves, suggest actions, reactions, and decisions. They are active links that create the story or narrative rather than just laying it out as a series of linear facts. Imagine the difference in something as simple as talking through your resume with someone with this approach! If we connect the pieces with "and then" we are simply reiterating what they could already understand from the resume. If we activate it with "therefores" and "buts" and the like, we ignite a story. We start to create a sense of how and why it unfolded, not merely that it did. We show when and how and why we made decisions, which is our best predictor of success in the next opportunity.

So, where do you begin? How do you frame or understand your own personal and professional development from a third person perspective? How to you objectify it and quantify it creatively? How do you start connecting it more intentionally and actively?

1. Build Your Skills

It starts with paying attention to what skills you are developing and experiences you are accumulating. If you can write well, it doesn't matter what context you are in. You have a valuable skill! If you are a good communicator, can build partnerships, can manage diverse groups, you have skills that are important anywhere! If you have created something from nothing, faced a blank canvas, initiated a program, developed a curriculum, or started a company, you have experience that is in short supply. You have to know what skills you have and how to use your experiences to explain how they are relevant to others.

2. Craft, Draft, and Re-craft
You should always be thinking of who you are and where you are going. Tell yourself. Practice telling others when they ask what you "do." Otherwise, someone else may answer that for you. You should think, for example, about how you have related to diverse audiences, seized new opportunities, or how your skills could be transferable to a variety of contexts. Again, it's your narrative and you are in control not only of how it develops but how it is communicated.

3. Sell Yourself
Don't get squeamish on me here! You aren't crafting your narrative just to talk to yourself. Many people cringe at the idea of selling themselves. It feels gross, especially for those like our Americorps Vistas who are doing work with their hearts first. But, the reality is, if you can't sell yourself then people aren't going to buy. Or, they are going to buy based on their perception of you rather than your reality. They will put you in a box that fits their need, which could keep you perpetually in an unsatisfying relationship to your job – i.e. it will never align fully with your work.

And, underlying it all: iterate! Personal and professional development is a process and so is building your narrative. Like everything else, you must invest continuously to keep from stagnating. You have to commit to reflecting on who you are, what you are doing, and who and what you are becoming. You must be organized, thinking about what skills you want to develop further and what you might be missing in terms of experiences. You need vision. And finally, you have to invest in your self relentlessly and humbly, both in terms of internal and spiritual development as well as supportive relationships.

"Managing the gap between vision and work, which often looks to others like being swallowed by failure, is a lifelong process. It is perhaps the one thing that any artist or innovator can control."[31]

You have to see yourself as a whole, as a system, and create and craft your narrative accordingly.

There is a famous painting by Edgar Degas called the Absinthe Drinker that, in its formal aspects, serves as a metaphor for making the connections in your own narrative – for crafting the whole. In it, a woman sits dejectedly with her head tilted slightly down behind a classic French café table. She sits strategically placed in the gap between two tables, seemingly belonging to neither. She's next to but uncomfortably disassociated from a gentleman sitting to her left. There is little more than a proximal connection between the two. Reaching

---

[31] Lewis, Sarah Elizabeth. *The Rise: Creativity, the Gift of Failure, and the Search for Mastery.* New York: Simon & Schuster, 2014. 57. Print.

toward the foreground is another table that extends off of the bottom of the canvas. It, like the other tables, is separated by a gap. A folded newspaper bridges the span of these two tables.

Viewed by one of Chatterjee's "visual ragpickers," the newspaper seems a benign detail, perhaps just an object suggesting familiarity and making the scene even more mundane. But, if you look at the image and use a finger to obscure the view of the newspaper (make it seem as if it weren't in the painting at all), the whole painting starts to fall apart. The newspaper is the lynchpin of the whole painting. It makes it all make sense. Without it, a mere visual accumulation of objects, the painting structurally falls apart like our non-Cezanne still life turned upside down.

The newspaper is the structural story of the painting that allows the rest of the viewing experience to unfold and be perceived by others as Degas intended.

As you think about your work as a system and as a whole, what's your newspaper?

Keep Your Eyes Up

So, here is my motivational moment for the book. For most of us, the opportunities we want don't just fall into our laps. We have to go create or find them. We have to believe we are the people to seize them, even when no one else believes we are. No one is out there looking for the candidate for their university or job or board of directors who doesn't make sense, who doesn't fit in a box. No one is looking to stick their neck out and put their reputation or job on the line to take a chance on you. Organizations and companies aren't in the business of making "risky" hires. You have to find the opportunity you want and either take the risk out of it for them or, better yet, show them how you are just the risk they need. You do that by having a solid grasp on and being able to communicate the whole of you.

Life

I want to wrap up this discussion of the whole on a much more personal note and share how seeing the whole can also be crucial to personal healing and resilience. All of us experience trauma and loss in life. It is part of being human. It is part of our narrative. But, so often we deal with it in isolation and see tragic moments as stand-alone events rather than culminating or touch-point moments in a larger process, a system, a whole.

When I was 16 years old, my father disappeared for several days. None of us knew where he was. I learned then, or at least it sunk in then, that he was severely Depressed and suicidal. His disappearance ultimately led him to check into a treatment facility for several months. He was not addicted. He was Depressed. Deeply.

As part of his time there, we all went out for "family week" to learn about his process of coping and healing and what role we could play in supporting him, while also taking care of ourselves. The first thing I remember, and honestly one of the few things I remember at all from the trip, was sitting as a family around my Dad and hearing him say: "For the last 20 years, I have wanted to jump off the Shelby Street Bridge."

Umph.

"Suicidal" is one thing. Hearing the details and the plan that could have happened any day for the last 20 years less than a mile from my house was another story. Hearing it from my Dad's mouth. Looking him in the eye. It was a total reality shifting moment.

14 years later, I received a call from my Mom asking if I could come over and sit with Dad. 30 years on the planet and I had never been called for this reason. He was Depressed. Sobbing. Couldn't get out of bed. So, I came home and sat with him. I held his hand as he sobbed with a brokenness you can only know if you hear and see it for yourself. It is not a cry I have heard anywhere else or from anyone else. I sat there. I tried to encourage him. Finally, I just sat there.

In the back of my mind, I knew it couldn't last. The sobbing being before me was not my Dad. He was somewhere else. Far away in time and space. What was before me was barely human, only an element, a mass, of purest sorrow. No real humanity left.

Two weeks later, a day before his 62nd birthday, April 27, 2006, my Dad went into Shelby Park (different from the bridge but still in my neighborhood), for years his "safe place" and refuge, a sacred place for my whole family, and put a bullet in his head.

There is too much for anyone to process in a time like this. You run through every aspect of your own life and relationships. You reassess your values. You wonder how you will care for your family. It is like every singular part of the complex system that is your life gets pulled apart and thrown into the air. There is no ground. No reality anymore. The whole is a pile of parts.

And, the inclination is to grab at pieces, to hold onto moments, to contrive explanations, narratives to obscure and obfuscate. We simplify, excuse, re-tell reality in a way that we can handle it in that moment, for that day. Whatever it takes. Ultimately, however, this piecemeal survival is unsustainable. We have to rebuild the whole.

"Seeing freshly starts with stopping our habitual ways of thinking and perceiving."[32]

I had to go back and understand my Dad as a complex human. I had to see him – as a whole. He was a successful attorney. A man of the people, an organizer and advocate. He was a champion of the underdog. He helped transform Nashville's inner city neighborhoods from violence and blight to thriving community. He was a Dad, a brother, a husband, and a son. He was also a man who survived childhood sexual abuse from a neighbor. He lived with that experience every day for 56 years even as his birth family denied its happening. Rejection. Conditional love. He was raised in a religion that was full of guilt and judgment. A defiled child, a shamed adult. He had severe clinical Depression that he

---

[32] Senge, Peter M. *Presence: Exploring Profound Change in People, Organizations, and Society.* New York: Doubleday, 2005. 29. Print.

recognized in his early 20's and that he had hidden from most of the world for 40 years. He was exhausted. And, ultimately, as he told us in his letter, he loved us but hated himself. So, what was he living for if he believed he was ruining our lives?

It was his spirit within. It's not that it was dead; it was corrupt, vicious, and destroying him from the inside. His suicide was the only way he saw left to rid himself and the world of that darkness.

I share this personal story because the understanding of the full picture of my Dad's life, of my life, is what allowed for healing to begin, and continue to this day and with this writing. No judgment. No excuses. No anger. All of those are elements of the struggle that I had to relinquish to accept the suffering, to start creating anew.

PART III:
CREATING

"Being done isn't the point. In fact, being done is the only thing to fear." – Seth Godin

"Where everything is already complete, there is no fulfillment." – John Dewey[33]

I don't remember months, perhaps even a whole year after Dad died. I experienced anxiety. I couldn't stand to be in crowds. I worked hard on my house and in my yard. I reflected constantly. Sometimes I sobbed uncontrollably. Sometimes I was fine.

I was not whole. I was struggling. Surviving. I didn't make art for three years, despite having a studio right there in my house and nothing else to keep me from it.

My artwork for several years up to that point had been technical, analytical, philosophical, and intentionally cold and emotionally vacuous. Conceptual. After Dad's death, I was not sure what creating artwork really meant to me anymore. I would rather just work in my yard, on my house, or do something else "practical" with my time. Creativity and art seemed unsubstantial, peripheral.

I entered my basement studio a few times, but I just stood there and looked around and was not compelled to engage. In retrospect, I believe all of my creative energy was focused on reinventing my self, getting to know my self, getting to know the world in a state that did not include the physical presence of my Dad. I had nothing else to create.

---

[33] Dewey, John. *Art as Experience*. New York: Perigee Books, 1980. 16. Print.

Then, in 2009, I went to New York and saw an exhibition of paintings by Francis Bacon. I came home. I started painting. It was as though I had no choice. I couldn't explain it. There were no words.

I had three years to reflect on. The painting process was cathartic. But, it also became sociological, philosophical, and psychological. I had fun. I made a mess. I cried. I laughed. I cranked Godsmack and Metallica. Intensity. I blasted Hank Jr. and Willie Nelson. Longing. I boomed Disturbed and Rage Against the Machine. Anger. I meditated with Pearl Jam. Indifference.

I lost 6 and 8 hours at a time rarely acknowledging my self, exhausted from three years of reflecting on my own existence. I just dialogued with the materials; they told me as much about where to go and what to do as I did them. I had no plan. I had no vision. It just kind of started happening.

As the process gave way to discernible thoughts, I began reflecting on my experience of loss and the physical and mental challenges, paradoxes, dislocations, and general contradictions of the trauma and reconstitution of it all. I woke up one day and my mind was ready to head into work and is energized to get back into the mix; my body felt like I had been hit by a truck. I woke up another day and was ready to start exercising, eating right, and getting my body back working for me again; my mind wanted me just to go back to sleep or just isolate in hopes that tomorrow it would feel clearer and more focused. I could read again, but I didn't want to talk about it. I could laugh again, but only around those I was most comfortable with. I could work again, but not in the same personal way I used to be able to. I was re-forming. I was still not whole.

Back and forth, on and on, my mind and my body distinguished themselves and their own mourning patterns and needs. I had no real control. It was a dissonance I had to learn to live with. By the time I started painting again, I didn't need to tell anyone; I just needed to "talk" about it. I didn't need anyone else to understand. I just needed to get something out. These paintings were for me. They were about me. They were about living.

As I finished new paintings and propped them up in corners and against walls, my studio became a chorus of new friends and philosophers, each talking with me and helping me explore further. Some had bad ideas and needed more work; some felt transcendent; others sat silently to speak to me another day, or perhaps never at all.

And after three more years of work, piles of work in my studio, my first child now a part of my life, I decided to put my art out there for others to see. It was time for someone else to have their own dialogue with my internal experiences and external manifestations, to interpret a language that I had created for myself and that was never necessarily intended for them. Some may have judged and despised them. They didn't speak to them. Some may have been engaged and asked questions. They provoked them. Some may have been moved and unable to say why.

I was conflicted in acknowledging that these paintings were for me, for my healing, my basic creativity, and that I wanted ultimately for someone else to find meaning in them.

This is why art matters. Francis Bacon didn't paint so that I might cope with suicide – create new life. He did it for his own reasons. Those musicians that soundtracked my painting process had no idea their art would be part of my healing.

In beginning to create again, I returned my self to process. I started putting energies into creating my life rather than just struggling with or against it. I began to reconstitute myself as a whole human. Becoming, again.

But, as creators, most of us are doing more than trying to become complete human beings. We are doing more than creating ourselves. We are making stuff. We are relating to the world through things we conjure and manifest. And, the world relates back to us, in part, through those things. This is what happened when I saw Francis Bacon, when I listened to my music while painting, when I looked at my own work in progress.

And while the concepts swirl and interact constantly and often indistinguishably, it is useful to distinguish between ourselves as creative beings (identity), our creative process (way of working) and our creative output (our work).

Much of what I have already discussed has been focused on the creative being, which I suggest entails becoming and requires seeing.

While common principles of creativity apply whether we are talking about our selves or something external we are making, there are unique elements of the creative process of the maker that provide that bridge between the self, the product, and the world.

"If personality is not what determines how creative we are, then what is? Research suggests that our habits of perception and thinking drive creativity more than some mysterious genetic trait – and habits are things we can do something about. Specifically, the power to be creative largely relies on three core components: Perception, Intellection (thinking), Expression."[34]

If the previous pages have mostly been devoted to perception and intellection, here I am more focused on expression. To be clear, these can only really be distinguished on paper and in principle, not really in practice. So, I delineate for the purposes of my own expression and clarity here.

With that in mind, to believe that our creative expression has value, we must first believe that the world around us is creative too. It too is in process. It is not complete. We are part of it. Otherwise, our personal expression would inevitably be redundant, or at least ancillary to the real world. Therefore, to keep creating, we have to believe that knowledge is also a process created collectively by humans and that we have something to contribute to it.

---

[34] Owens, David A. *Creative People Must Be Stopped 6 Ways We Kill Innovation (Without Even Trying)*. Somerset: Wiley, 2011. 28. Print.

It is "in the social experience of history that we as human beings have created knowledge. It's because of that that we continue to recreate the knowledge we created, and create a new knowledge. If knowledge can be overcome, if the knowledge of yesterday necessarily does not make sense today then I need another knowledge. It means that knowledge has *historicity*. That is, knowledge is never static. It's always in the process."[35]

Questioning

"Why do ducks have wings?" - My 3-year-old daughter

Creating new knowledge, then, creating anything for that matter, starts with asking questions: questioning the perceptions of others, the sources of accepted fact; questioning the thinking that verified it; questioning how and why it was manifest and distributed as fact. As creators, we deconstruct our surroundings in all forms to decide if we believe them, in them, as they are, or if they are as temporal and fallible as we are. Are there things to explore rather than merely accept? Presumably there are. Such is my faith in my own creativity.

Peter Thiel suggests: "That is what a startup has to do: question received ideas and rethink business from scratch." But, doing that well as a startup means doing it

---

[35] Horton, Myles, and Brenda Bell. *We Make the Road by Walking: Conversations on Education and Social Change*. Philadelphia: Temple UP, 1990. 194. Print.

well first in how you question "received ideas" wherever you experience them. Creativity is discipline.

It is difficult, if not impossible, to see the whole, whether in art, work, business, or life, if you don't question in this way. "Received ideas" are those projected to or upon us, sourced elsewhere, from others' perceptions and intellection. They are "wholes" in sheep's clothing! Everything around us that is constructed or impacted by humans is a reality made up of decisions. Those decisions continue to accumulate results over time until new decisions change their course. If we want to change something, then, we have to get to the source of the projection; see, question, and change that process that created it. What is its historicity? What was the original question? How did this become the accepted answer? Who are the players? What's the better question now?

A Question of Questions

Needless to say in the swirl of culture and crime and citizenship and crazy that I grew up in, I had a lot of questions as a kid. Why were some people homeless? Why did Boots talk to his elbow? What was AIDS and why were so many of our neighbors dying of it? Why did the preacher down the street decapitate the church janitor, cut off his tattoos, roll him up in a carpet, and burn the church down with him inside? You know, your standard kid questions! There was no way for me to process it all. There still really isn't. But, it was critical that each of my days as a child ended with a simple question from my Mom: Do you have any questions?

If I offered and left this question-of-questions lingering amongst a group with no other context, most of us would sit in confused, uncomfortable silence until one brave soul finally asked "about what"?

Do you have any questions?

These five simple words were the last thing I heard every night as a child as my Mom tucked me in to bed. I never once asked "about what"? Even as a child, I knew my Mom was asking me a sincere and open-ended question. Some nights I might just reply "no" and drift off to sleep. Other nights, I might have a question about school, about the homeless friend passed out on our doorstep, about why my grandmother died. I remember once even asking what the "f-word" meant (I heard it from my Dad) – objectively and rationally Mom informed me (the life sciences version); no taboo, no shame.

Mom had asked me a question and was willing to answer, or help me find the answer, whatever may come. We had the complete, encyclopedic Life Cycle book series as backup! She was also willing to say when she didn't have the answer, or perhaps there was no answer. No bullshit just because I was a kid.

The important thing, though, is that there was no "about what." Mom's question was not loaded with the parameters of her comfort or her knowledge base. She wasn't fishing for particular information. She wasn't framing my response by the nature of her question.

Being asked a genuine, open-ended question every night as I fell asleep meant that genuine questioning became natural to me, curiosity cultivated. In fact, it meant that questioning was a driver of my personal development and even more questioning the inevitable result. Questioning was instilled as an ethic rather than merely a practice. When I am at my best, questioning illuminates my personal and professional relationships and guides the way I approach the world around me. Alternatively, when I start dealing in answers, something is terribly wrong. I know I am not myself, and I'm certainly not being creative.

After all, asking questions is about engaging life. Reflection. Curiosity. Sourcing creativity. It's about showing respect for others' experiences, knowledge, and opinions. Humility. It's about exploring and learning. Growth. It's about staying intellectually and spiritually invested. Hungry. It's about being an artist, a friend, a partner.

A question then is not merely the absence of an answer. It's the start of the creative process.

But, for adults, the question is too often fleeting. "As everyday life becomes more jam-packed with tasks, activities, diversions, and distractions, "stepping back and questioning" is unlikely to get a slot on the schedule. Which means some of the most important questions – about why we're engaging in all those activities in the first place – never get raised."[36]

---

[36] Berger, Warren. *A More Beautiful Question: The Power of Inquiry to Spark Breakthrough Ideas*. New York: Bloomsbury USA, 2014. 77. Print.

When our life is filled with tasks and to-dos such that we feel we have limited time for other things, we say we are busy. Alternately, when our life is filled with creative activity, even when we still feel we have limited time for other things, we feel productive. And, the cult of the busy can quickly and easily drown out the creativity within each of us by stealing our focus and energy and minimizing our space for reflection and regeneration.

Organizations

This reality is as true for organizations and companies as it is for us as individuals. "When it comes to questioning, companies are like people: They start out doing it, then gradually do it less and less. A hierarchy forms, a methodology is established, and rules are set; after that, what is there to question?"[37]

In the now classic business book <u>The Innovator's Dilemma</u>, Clayton Christensen distinguishes two types of technological innovation that I think apply to this discussion: 1. Sustaining innovation and 2. Disruptive innovation. Each starts with a different set of questions.

Christensen characterizes sustaining innovation: "What all sustaining (innovations) have in common is that they improve the performance of established products, along the dimensions of performance…that have (been) historically valued."[38] It asks: How do we

---

[37] Berger, Warren. *A More Beautiful Question: The Power of Inquiry to Spark Breakthrough Ideas*. New York: Bloomsbury USA, 2014. 20. Print.
[38] Christensen, Clayton M. *The Innovator's Dilemma: When New Technologies Cause Great Firms to Fail*. Boston, Mass.: Harvard Business School, 2000. XV. Print.

improve upon what we already have or are already doing?

In other words, sustaining innovation reinforces existing value structures, and incrementally improves our performance on the things we already think matter. It facilitates, rather than changes, our fundamental processes. Sustaining innovation actually reinforces the current system; it doesn't question it.

On the other hand, disruptive innovation redefines "performance trajectories" and dimensions of success. It alters the systemic variables that we deem important, redefines our processes, illuminates nuances in our outcomes, or changes them altogether. It questions the system. It seeks to change the system.

For Christensen, the "dilemma" is that sustaining innovations please our current customers and feed our bottom line. They are validating. They feel good to us. They don't require a lot of change. So, we invest in them heavily, if not exclusively. Disruptive innovations, on the other hand, are rarely, if ever, "asked for," can feel very scary and chaotic, and initially often underperform sustaining innovations - that is, until they make them obsolete. So, we don't invest in them.

Now, obviously, we don't just wake up one morning and say "this seems like a good day to create disruptive innovation". Most of us don't anyway. If it were that easy, it wouldn't be all that disruptive. We can, however, create environments where disruptive innovation can be cultivated and surfaced, environments where we learn and iterate as individuals and as organizations and companies.

"All organizations are organic and perishable. They are created by people and they need to be constantly recreated if they are to survive."[39]

But, most of us don't live and work in environments that are so actively and thoroughly recreating themselves, disrupting their own practices. As humans, we work hard to create and build systems and organizations, but somewhere along the line, we forget that we are the ones that built them, that they reflect our questions and represent our decisions. Our organizations begin to create (or destroy) us when we forget that fact. Companies and organizations take on a life of their own. "They" start making decisions. "They" start doing things to us. We defer the "them" for the answers. We stop recreating them for ourselves. We lose the question of why we built them, or why we joined them, in the first place.

Public school systems are a great example of organizations that have failed over time to keep recreating themselves. Now, it's not difficult to argue that the history of public education was never really about the student. That argument is largely moot for my purposes here. The reality is that if you talk to any teacher or principal today, they will probably sincerely tell you that "it's all about the students" even if the pedagogy, schedule, and class structure suggest

---

[39] Robinson, Ken. *Out of Our Minds: Learning to Be Creative*. Fully Rev. and Updated ed. Oxford: Capstone, 2011. 12. Print.

otherwise. These fundamental structures to the organization of schools are largely established as fact. They long ago stopped being processes to be created and recreated as the purpose of education evolved along with the economy and culture. We stopped asking how and if schooling is actually a process that supports education as a process that supports learning.

In fact, it's one of the few elements of modern society where I could take a teenager from today's times and have them talk to my great grandparents about education and they would still totally understand what they were talking about. Yes, technology has impacted education, but kids still are organized by age into buildings that have rooms that are constructed around subjects with an "expert" teacher at the front and kids in desks capturing and regurgitating information. Do you realize how much more we know about the brain and how kids learn than we did when we designed this?

But, we train teachers based on this established structure. We create student disciplinary systems to reinforce the structure. We generate, deliver, and assess content based on this structure. We establish policies and handbooks and professional expectations that conform to this structure. And, I guess the simplest question is: If we started from scratch and wanted the kids of today to master certain areas of content and become lifelong learners, is this what we would design?

In 13 years, I have never met anyone who would say "yes" to this question.

The Policy Lobotomy

And, it's not just education. I recognize that's an easy punching bag, and don't want to lose my point because of it. This sort of calcification starts to happen any place where humans organize. During an entrepreneurship workshop (a couple of years after I had him in my "Launching the Venture" class), Michael Burcham proclaimed: "Every time you make a policy for something that is common sense, you take a little piece of everybody's brain."

I chuckled at the candor (and the image), but have been digesting it ever since, wondering where all it applied, including public education.

Common sense is typically understood as a base intellectual or intuitive state that generates common knowledge, something we all basically agree on. It's common, baseline, understood. But, common sense can also be the question we want and need to ask, not just a bit of common information. "Those with common sense not only ask the correct questions but also question the very premise from which their questions come."[40] It suggests common interpretation, decision-making, and process of evaluation. Common sense presumes shared values. It presumes common commitments.

And so, it turns out that common sense isn't all that common or basic. It is complex and ever changing. And, when organizations stop investing in common vision and values, creating a common narrative, and replace it

---

[40] Chatterjee, Debashis. *Leading Consciously a Pilgrimage toward Self-mastery.* Boston, Mass.: Butterworth-Heinemann, 1998. 17. Print.

with policymaking – common rules and regulations - they head down a dark road that ultimately chokes common anything. They stop questioning, codify their expectations, and narrow their avenues for creativity and innovation.

It seems to me that organizational policy, best used, establishes a safety net for the organization (or a community of people of any sort for that matter). It sort of says: if our people or our actions fall below this basic level, or beyond this broad range of acceptable behavior, then there will be consequences. If there are uncertainties for the individual member where he needs guidance from the organization, there it is.

In these cases, policy is intended to be behind-the-scenes and not an explicit part of everyday interactions (except for the HR directors and the like who manage them for the organization). Policy should provide a baseline, or set of parameters, that most successful employees don't spend much time hovering around.

But, for many, particularly larger organizations, instead of providing broad parameters, policy is perceived to define the accepted level of execution. It has moved from covering the organization for the worst-case scenario to codifying expectations of daily performance. So, people at a decisive moment defer to policy rather than their common sense or creativity.

And, this, according to Burcham, is where we lose a piece of our brain, and (according to me) our soul. It's where organizations lose their innovation.

So, we must decide if we want to create policy-driven or people-driven organizations (or likely an effective balance of both). The former leverages the tools of the organization; the latter the tools and creativity of all of its members. The former slows and systematizes organizational function; the latter helps it remain nimble and open to new inputs. Either in the extreme exposes the organization and its members to a different set of threats.

Which brings me to another quote from Burcham that day: "Your people should grow at a faster rate than your company."

So, there is the real challenge! When you look at your company or your organization or your community, are the people who make it up growing faster than the entity as a whole? Are they pushing you for new opportunities for personal growth? Can they execute without micromanagement? Do they surprise you with their creativity? Are they generating innovation and developing ideas to drive you forward? Or, are they waiting on direction? Acting only if policy is there to guide them?

If it's the latter, they may have experienced what, based on Burcham's imagery, I call a policy lobotomy.

To avoid this unfortunate procedure, we have to be deliberate about facilitating environments where we all can continue questioning and creating. This isn't about chaos, or about my 3 year old who asks "why" to everything to the point that we can sometimes do nothing else. It's about being open to what Cathy

Johnson describes as "wandering – but with a conscious step."[41]

Creative Tension

Ultimately, good questions create tension. The context of those questions and how they are received will determine if it is creative tension or potentially destructive tension.

I first read about the idea of creative tension in Peter Senge's The Fifth Discipline and explored it further over the years through the work of Robert Fritz – who Senge references. When I read it the first time, I was in the midst of trying to engage a group of 15 teens in work to improve conditions in their community. I was trying to develop and empower them as advocates and activists to help improve educational and economic opportunities for themselves and their families.

And yet, the reality was, they didn't see, couldn't see, any other way than "the way it is." They knew their life, their family, their neighborhood, and for the most part that was that. If I asked them to imagine their lives being different, they looked at me untrustingly. They had asked or been asked that before, and they had either been laughed at or lied to. So, they stopped imagining something "more." They stopped creating. Several of the young men articulated that they had never expected to live, or at least not outside of jail, until they were 18

---

[41] Barron, Frank. *Creators on Creating: Awakening and Cultivating the Imaginative Mind.* New York: Putnam, 1997. 30. Print.

years old anyway. Community? Change? How about just survival!

One day, we were exploring the topic of violence in school. I don't recall, but I suspect there had been a fight at school that day, the police had been called out, the day disrupted, and they all needed some time to process and debrief. By this time, the group had gotten pretty used to me asking "why" no matter what they said. I invoked my inner 3-year old 23 years late and a decade before my daughter turned it back on me again. In fact, I had even done a workshop with them on why "why" was the most important word in the English language. It wasn't until years later in business school that I found out that "The 5 Whys" is a known root cause technique supposedly created by Toyota Motor Corporation. Who knew!? Anyway, I had asked enough whys that one young man said "because there will just always be violence in schools!" The others agreed. It wasn't even a consideration. There was no creative tension around the idea. There was no sense that there was something even to change. It was destructive tension cloaked as apathy.

So, I simply asked if they thought that schools in a neighboring county, wealthier, whiter, more educated, suburban, had the same kind of violence they had in their schools. Unanimously, but somewhat reluctantly, they all said "no." I let them sit in silence for a prolonged pause. So, violence wasn't inevitable. If it wasn't inevitable in these other communities, then it wasn't inevitable. Violence had to be an effect of larger systemic, community issues. We couldn't address violence without addressing those.

This was only one of many topics that we had to move from the inevitable column to the changeable, from the apathetic to the actionable, from internalized oppression to liberation, from the known fact to the controllable variable. Peter Block would suggest we had to change the conversation: "The future of a community then becomes a choice between a retributive conversation (a problem to be solved) and a restorative conversation (a possibility to be lived into)."[42]

In doing so, we introduced some creative tension back into their lives. We had to move from people who were acted upon to becoming actors ourselves, from the victims of personal and community conditions to the creators of a new kind of community. So, literally the day after I read Senge's description of creative tension, I took a giant rubber band to work with me, the kind you use to rehab a sprained ankle. I wanted to show my youth what energy looked like, what creative tension could look like in Senge's model. I wanted to show them through a visual and kinesthetic demonstration how defining a desired future state was necessary to create its possibility. By the way, I also had these young people read other excerpts from the 5th Discipline and discuss how it applied to their lives and work.

When all the young people were together, I asked one young man to hold the rubber band at one end. He stood there with a royal blue rubber band drooping sadly to

---

[42] Block, Peter. *Community: The Structure of Belonging*. San Francisco: Berrett-Koehler, 2008. 53. Print.

the floor at his feet. I asked the group what it was. They looked at me like I was crazy, which I was used to by this point, as were they. After they wrongly stated that it was a rubber band, I told them "NO! This is your life; this is you!"

There are some benefits to already being considered a slightly crazy white dude.

I picked up the other end of the rubber band and stood next to the young man and began asking him a series of questions about his life, about what he wanted to do, be, become? With every answer he gave, I asked him to take a step further away from me until the two of us stood with a taut rubber band between us. The unsure participant and his peer onlookers were getting nervous that someone was about to get popped! It was palpable.

So, I asked again, what is this?

I flicked the taut rubber band with my free hand. It bounced up and down. I pulled it toward the audience, still holding it firmly in my other hand, and let it go making an audible pop. It was tension. It was energy. It was sound. It had capacity to act and react to things happening to it, around it.

How is it different than when the band was dangling at the young man's feet when we started? Why was it different? What had made it so?

In this scenario, this young man responding to my prompts began to articulate a vision for his future, his life, relationships, and opportunities. As he articulated that future, I had him take steps away from me. I represented his present. In his answers, he began to create tension between his present state and future vision. But, it was only his vision of his own future that could create tension and generate the energy to make it reality. I couldn't create it for him. That future, in turn, gave him a context and a direction for making decisions and investing his energy in the present. This may seem simple and obvious, but transforming that future state from something that would just happen to something that could be created is a crucial step toward liberation. It is the first step toward claiming power over our lives and therefore owning them.

I used this exercise for years to generate the same type of conversations and introduce this mental model to young people and adults across the country. And, as a result, I began to recognize when and where others were using it in their own ways without even knowing it.

A couple of years later, building on the college access advocacy of this same group of young people, I worked with some colleagues to design and fund a college access center for low-income, first generation students, the first and only of its kind in Nashville. Fundamental to the vision was not merely the attainment of a credential, although that was key for many of our youth in attempting to escape poverty, but extending a vision of the future to give meaning and focus to the present. Creative tension. What aspiration do they have beyond high school that would help them stay motivated and making good decisions in high school?

So, we wanted a college access center that was developmentally and culturally sound, built around true choice, and power and vision of young people. A couple of years after we finally got the Nashville College Connection off the ground we hired a friend and colleague named Jeff Dotts as the new director. We knew he "got it." It wasn't about paperwork or test scores or credentials. It was first about vision; it had to be. And, as he brought his unique approach to the work, he also institutionalized with his staff of mentors a very simply question for the students: what do you want your life to look like when you are 40? This was question #1. In fact, that was the only question that mattered until the students could start to answer it.

Remember, some of these kids never imagined turning 18! Almost all of them would be the first in their family to go to college. They were going way out on a limb and needed to know and own for themselves why they were doing it. They couldn't just be getting pushed. This deep personal knowledge of "why" is what could keep them focused when times got challenging, when they inevitably failed at something new and difficult. The personal, cultural, and academic transition to college is all about the new and difficult. So, failure on many levels is inevitable.

Myles Horton, founder of the Highlander Research and Education Center, reinforces the need for pushing this life horizon, even indefinitely, and emphasizes the role failure has to play: "I've always thought it was important to persuade people to be willing to fail because if you're not willing to fail, you'll always choose easy goals. Your sights are limited by what you do. The pursuit of an expanding, unrestricted goal that is always receding in front of you, as you get a clearer view of where you're going or would like to, is not an experience to shun."[43]

Renown painter James Rosenquist summarizes and offers a twist on this reality from the artist's perspective: (Making art) is working like hell towards something you know nothing about."[44]

Again, Jeff didn't ask them what they wanted to "do" when they grow up. He didn't ask what they wanted to be. He didn't ask them where they wanted to go to college or how they were going to pay for it. None of these mattered except in the context of a future that they could define for themselves. It had to be their future, owned in their present. Jeff's question helped establish a horizon to generate the creative tension necessary to keep teenagers focused on a laborious, long, tedious, and bureaucratic system of college admissions and financial aid, not to mention completing high school successfully. But, with a sense of their future, they could own their own process. No blaming teachers. No blaming counselors. Self-advocacy. Ownership. It was their creative tension now.

As a counter point to this approach, we would frequently hear students say something like: "Oh, Mrs. So-and-So already got me into X school." We knew that kid probably wouldn't make it. Mrs. So-and-So wasn't going to be there with him to register for classes or deal

---

[43] Horton, Myles, and Judith Kohl. *The Long Haul: An Autobiography.* New York: Doubleday, 1990. 176. Print.
[44] Findlay, Michael. *The Value of Art: Money, Power, Beauty.* Munich: Prestel, 2012. 175. Print.

with a roommate or study for that first college test. And, he had abdicated the process and the ownership of making it to college to her.

Even when I was in business school, the importance of this kind of individual creative tension was fundamental. Just like at Cranbrook, it was clear who was at Owen to learn and grow and who was there for other reasons. Some were doctors frustrated with the way the business of healthcare was run and wanted to create a different future. Some worked in large companies and felt they could create a pathway forward with a few more skills and experiences. Regardless of the specific motivation or context, most of my classmates were driven by a sense of future they wanted to create and own.

Still there were a few who seemed to be there because they didn't know what else to do. They were stuck and hoped an MBA would help them get unstuck. It was pretty clear after two long years who those people were! They had largely thrown in the towel. Merely getting unstuck was no longer creating sufficient tension to get them through the grueling two years of life and coursework. They were getting an MBA to solve a problem, rather than to create a future.

As I observed and applied it over time, however, this individualized conception of creative tension was just that: individual. It was foundational, but didn't say much about how we generate creativity when we have to work with and through others. Over the years, I had learned that I almost always did my work with and through others.

What I didn't realize initially was that the power of the creative tension I was attempting to create among my group of youth was not just between them and their future. It was a tension we were co-creating and inviting others to co-create and co-own as part of our relationship and our work together. All of those who observed the process and heard the future vision of the young man in my example were now a part of a system to support and hold him accountable for creating it. After all, we were at our core a group of individuals who sought community change – something much bigger than an individual. Alone, we lacked the support and insight to sustain us when we walked out on that edge. Alone, we could be marginalized, isolated. En masse, we could not be silenced.

Perhaps most importantly, alone we lack critical feedback on our choices, gentle reminders on our direction, and general accountability to a vision we told others was important to us. We need others because it is too easy to make excuses and get lost in our own selves, self-marginalized by the limitations of our own thinking, obsessions, and delusions.

David Foster Wallace: "A huge percentage of the stuff that I tend to be automatically certain of is, it turns out, totally wrong and deluded. Here's one example of the utter wrongness of something I tend to be automatically sure of: Everything in my own immediate experience supports my deep belief that I am the absolute center of the universe, the realest, most vivid and important person in existence...Think about it: There is no experience you've had that you were not at the absolute center of. The world as you experience it is right there in front of you, or behind you, to the left or right of you, on your TV, or your monitor, or whatever. Other people's thoughts and feelings have to be communicated to you somehow, but your own are so immediate, urgent, real -- you get the idea.[45]

In this kind of isolation of the self, there is no creative tension outside of the self. In fact, when the self is left in such isolation for too long, it can be incredibly destructive. Despite his insights and literary brilliance, or perhaps because of them, Wallace ultimately committed suicide.

The fact is that we need relationships. And, more times than not, those relationships are how we get our best and most important work done. They are how we create and demonstrate our best selves. Sharing our aspirations brings others into them with us. Finding the person or group of people to share our dreams with can provide the strength and validation we need to start acting on and creating them – and helping others create theirs. Most of us think our dreams, or even the problems we dream to get beyond, are ours alone. We think that we are the crazy ones, or perhaps the only ones dealing in self-doubt or feeling marginalized. But, of course, we are not. We find safety in common

---

[45] https://www.youtube.com/watch?v=IYGaXzJGVAQ

experiences and power in shared dreams, which can set the stage for transformative, creative action.

Relating to others and the world with this sort of transparency, even relating personally to our own deepest desires and visions, requires not only humility but also the ability to take risks. Emotional risks. Relationship risks. Personal and professional risks. Risk is a form of creative tension. It isn't something to be avoided. It starts with being open to risk individually and then opening to the power of sharing that risk with a group or team of others.

On the individual front, Chris Rock puts it exactly like Chris Rock would put it: "You've got to make yourself scared. When I did that play not too long ago, it was like, Oh, this shit is scary. I'm out of my comfort zone. I'm the low man on the totem pole. I could really suck at this. But it's in moments like that that you are going to learn the most…It scared me and I did some things that sucked. But you learn more from fucking up than you do from success, unfortunately. And failure, if you don't let it defeat you, is what fuels your future success."[46]

Comfort, Risk, Danger

Before we can work with others beyond their comfort zone, we have to get out of ours. In that light, I learned a group training/facilitation protocol many years ago simply called Comfort/Risk/Danger.

---

[46] Apatow, Judd. *Sick in the Head: Conversations about Life and Comedy.* New York: Random House, 2015. 70. Print.

When working with a team, the protocol helps them, based loosely around whatever it is they are trying to accomplish and what kind of work it entails, to share what things put them as individuals in the comfort zone, the risk zone, or the danger zone.

We mark three large, concentric circles on the floor, usually with masking tape. The smallest circle, the bull's eye, is the danger zone. The next ring out creates the risk zone and the outermost is the comfort zone. We then read statements pertinent to their work. This could be around workplace safety, culture, climate, project management, finances, or anything else that would feel a realistic element to the work we were trying to accomplish together. Based on the statement, each person steps into the zone that statement puts them in. We then ask people in each zone to share why they chose to step into that particular circle.

Some team members will be totally comfortable with public speaking; for others, it feels dangerous. For some, crunching numbers is comfortable; for others, it would be a risk. Some have never worked with diverse populations and find the unknown of it dangerous. Some find it risky. Some find conflict dangerous; some find it risky. And, we all know those who are a little too comfortable with it.

But, we need speakers; we need numbers people; we need people who create, manage, and support effective conflict. And, we cannot afford for those skill sets to reside with one person or in one department. It's too easy for them to get marginalized, or to go away completely. Some element of each has to be part of a broader team dynamic.

We also need people who are actively learning, and humans learn better, and are therefore more creative, when there is some level of risk. In the risk zone, we are stretching, challenging ourselves, and actively asking questions and seeking solutions. When we are comfortable, on the other hand, we are surrounded by what we already know. We are passive. When we are in danger, we aren't learning either (social, emotional, and professional danger; not just physical). Fight or flight kicks in. We shut down, seek relief, and avoid (or project our danger onto others).

The fact is that people in the comfort zone are dangerous to our organizations. Organizations stop learning and adapting comfort zone by comfort zone. Alternately, people in the danger zone are also dangerous to our organizations. They not only aren't helping us learn but can easily transition to an active threat to the learning of others.

So, the Comfort/Risk/Danger protocol helps groups reflect individually and relate that to the overall work of the team. It generates a new frame for the idea of risk that in most organizations gets misconstrued as a negative or destructive force. The protocol also helps generate a conversation about building an effective team, not just by capitalizing on what everyone is already good at (i.e. what puts them in the comfort zone). There is no creativity there. Creating an effective team is about learning how to support a pervasive element of risk.

While I have facilitated this process many times, I have never felt its challenge personally quite like I did with Zeumo. For starters, I had been an artist, organizer, youth worker, educational consultant, and trainer: what the hell did I know about technology? Much less creating it? Is it smart to found your first startup when you are in your late thirties and have an infant? What about having a second child while you're at it? We have how much cash on hand? So, that's like how many weeks/months before we run out?

And, that's just on the individual front. Everyone else on the team had their own version of these questions and other issues that could very easily put us all in danger. So, how does a startup team like us support each other to keep it risky?

Startup Tension

Many, if not most, startups fail because the founding team implodes in some form or fashion. Presumably, by its nature, a startup begins with creative tension. There is an idea and a team that buys into it. There are investors and potential clients. You start creating. The energy is palpable.

This is how Zeumo started. And, then, we beta tested the original education product in high schools, which is to say we tested an incomplete idea and untested technology with a bunch of teenagers and teachers. Let's just say that our creative tension was put to the test. Every day I went to work wondering who and how many people were going to proverbially kick me in the balls that day. What didn't work? Why didn't it do this or that? Why are we even doing this? Who asked for this? Where's the Zumba class?!

It sucked. Bad. And, it put extraordinary pressure on us as a team. We were still learning how to work with each other, and now we were collectively getting the shit kicked out of us. So, in response, initial vision and product directions start to diverge. Creative differences show themselves. Differences in how people respond to stress start to show. Strategic differences unfold. Different interpretations of the product and the direction develop. The job of sales is to say "yes" and the job of product management is to be more discerning – and say "no" a lot. Perhaps, you're at the mercy of engineers. Suddenly, the team is blanketed in potentially destructive tension.

This evolution is a reality of working together and adapting to evolving goals, feedback, and shared (or not) learning. And, it's not just startups. How many bands flame out after that first album? They almost always attribute it to "creative differences." The people change. The environment changes. The product changes. There's just a lot of room for creative differences! This is the beauty and the challenge of team dynamics, particularly in a creative environment, where we have to be so deeply invested in each other and the product to survive.

There's a great model for understanding this kind of evolving team dynamic, whether in a startup, a band, or pretty much any group anywhere. It's called Tuckman's

Stages of Group Development, and it includes four main stages: Forming, Storming, Norming, and Performing. And, it's important to note that Tuckman emphasizes in the model that all of these stages are both necessary and inevitable. They happen in cycles and repeat themselves. They aren't linear. They're relational, temporal, and contextual.

As a leader, I help form a team (it doesn't really matter for what for these purposes but clearly the team itself needs to know why they were formed!). When they meet and get to know each other, there is some newness and excitement and energy in the experience and in the promise of their work together (forming). Then the ideas start flowing. Different perspectives start to emerge. Conflicts start to surface. Communication challenges begin (storming). And, depending on how intense all of this is, the group may have to return to the forming stage, or best-case take the deliberate steps of establishing some norms and working toward those.

Let's assume the latter. So, now people have some expectations of each other both in terms of deliverables and how they will work together, communicate, and so forth. They know each other better, so they develop tolerance for each other's quirks and communication styles. Things become less personal and more focused on accomplishing the work (norming). In some strange world that I have never experienced, the group could translate this directly into the performing stage. In reality, however, they are much more likely to hit some snags, return to storming for a while, and then try norming again. Again, this sort of pattern of group development is not only to be expected, but is required. Additionally, groups don't work in a vacuum. So, if a group brings in new members, the stages will shift again. If their goals or timelines evolve, the stages may shift again.

In performing, the team starts to work as a unit to achieve their goals. This includes keeping each other focused, motivated, and understanding and working with individual's various strengths and weaknesses.

No team stays in any one stage perpetually. If we stay in forming too long, we lose clarity and motivation. If we stay in storming too long, we implode or otherwise destroy ourselves. If we stay in norming, we never get anything done and end up a team for the sake of a team. Performing constantly at a high is simply not a human reality, much less one of a group of humans.

Understanding a framework like Tuckman's is a great way to objectify where we are as a group and support having difficult conversations. It helps neutralize the emotions and interpersonal dynamics that have us in whichever stage we are in at any given time. And, whether we use a model like this or just sense it and work through it otherwise, we have to survive the storm. We can't stay there. And, we have to do better than temporary reprieve or ignoring issues and hoping they will go away. We have to be able to establish some spoken and unspoken norms. This is the only chance we have to sustain any kind of performance over time.

But, this is why, in the startup world, what we hear over and over again, particularly from angel investors, is that they are investing in the team as much or more than the idea or product. They all know that the idea we have in our first pitch decks will never be executed as we are presenting it to them. It will have to adapt and change as we learn more about the market, the customer, the technology, and so forth. We will have to iterate. And, if our team can't do that and stick together then we aren't worth investing in.

Even as Zeumo was in the process of being acquired, our team dynamic was a primary interest. There's a lot of good technology out there. There's obviously a lot of bad stuff too. But, by the time you are talking acquisition, you figure the latter has been sussed out and left behind. So, as the acquiring company was looking at technologies to buy, they were really looking at the team and the approach to see how it would mesh with the larger company. Where were we on Tuckman's model? Where had we been? How did we work together now? How did leadership work and communicate with each other? What was the overall culture? In other words, how were we navigating the tension of being a startup and continuing to create our product? Were we still creative or were we at each other's throats?

A Relational Tension Model

So, all of this leads me to rethinking creative tension as I have learned it and used it to date. I wanted to create a model that seemed more applicable to my work, to my real world. So, obviously, this means to my relationships.

When I look at creative organizations and leaders and compare them to the ones that are less creative, what is the difference? How can we understand where and how we gain or lose creativity so that we can better lead and manage creatively?

I'll start by returning to the front lines of education: the student/teacher relationship. While there are plenty of creative teachers and plenty of creative students in schools and classrooms across the country, how many of them are deploying their creativity together? Even if they are creative individuals, how creative are their relationships?

Let's return to the rubber band visual. Instead of the two ends being held between a student's current state and his future self, as in my previous example, imagine a student and a teacher are holding opposite ends of a rubber band. Imagine the same alternative school teachers I asked to draw success for their students on one side with their students on the other. The rubber band, instead of representing the relationship between the present and future self, represents that relationship between two people. The actions of each affect the relationship. As each pulls away or comes closer, the tension in the band changes. It moves. It makes sound. It has energy.

But, if one pulls too hard, the energy generates fear and uncertainty in the other (What happens if she lets go? I'm gonna get popped!). Movement becomes limited. The energy becomes bound. The band is taut. It is not productive. This is destructive tension, over-tension.

Now, what happens if one relaxes the tension on his end? He disinvests in the relationship. The band goes limp. It has no energy, no sound, no movement. It sags. What does this mean for the one left holding it? What about the one who let go? This lack of shared tension (energy) results in destructive tension, under-tension.

In a creative relationship, the energy each person contributes is dynamic and dependent upon each individual's personal goals, their shared goals, their relationship and their trust in each other. It is constantly changing. It requires vigilance and investment. So, to remain productive, we have to constantly communicate the tension we need and listen to others as they do the same. We push and pull each other. We know when the other needs to release the tension. We communicate when we need to. We know when someone dropped his end. Our relationships must become more dynamic and multifaceted such that the right tension becomes both intentional and intuitive. Imagine a creative relationship you have or have had that's focused on a goal, creating something together. Reflect on when it has worked well or when it has faltered. Now, imagine you and your partner(s) on the opposite ends of this rubber band and use it to picture the creative energy you generate in that band. How did it change over time? Why? How did you lose creative energy? Get it back?

The space between us and the relationships we leverage to create our world is dynamic and full of tension. That's what gives us the energy to create. And, while my example here has been those relationships that are closest to us, most creative in our day-to-day lives, Martin Luther King Jr. describes this relational tension model us a basic tenet of all life: "All this is simply to say that all life is interrelated. We are caught in an inescapable network of mutuality; tied in a single garment of destiny. Whatever affects one directly, affects all indirectly...Strangely enough, I can never be what I ought to be until you are what you ought to be. You can never be what you ought to be until I am what I ought to be."

I can't imagine articulating more possibility for creative tension than those last two sentences. I call them the "oughts" when I use this quote in workshops. I repeat them a couple of times for emphasis. It's an extraordinary thought, potentially too grand in scale to conceive the full implications.

But, the "oughts" start with our most immediate relationships – these are our controllable variables. How can we develop more mutually creative relationships? Improve the ones we have? What are the key differences between a relationship that produces destructive tension and one that generates creative tension? I suggest these elements are a place to start:

Shared Purpose
A truly common purpose is an extraordinary thing. And, too often, we assume a common purpose with others because of the nature of the organization we work in, proximity, our socio-economic similarities, or perhaps even the community we live in. But, a common purpose

can never be taken for granted. It must be overt. It must be ever-present. A common purpose is extremely hard to develop, much less maintain. Like the creative tension that generates it, common purpose requires vigilance to keep adapting it over time while reinventing and continuously communicating and reflecting on its current form.

Sports teams are probably our culture's most obvious example of this concept. We have all seen the teams that are loaded with talent, whether in little league or the NFL, that just don't seem to win. They do well, but they get surprised or "upset" year after year by some other team not many people were paying attention to. Alternatively, there are teams who rarely have the most talent but always seem to win. The old trite saying that there is "no I in team" holds true. If there is an "I" then at least one player is working for a different purpose. That may not matter for a while, but it will matter critically at the time we need to be a team the most.

Ownership of the Work
Ownership boils down to how we carry that sense of shared purpose as part of who we are and what we are about, even when no one is looking. Too many people want to own the outcomes, but aren't willing to own the work. So, where does that shared purpose live for us? How is it manifest in the work we are doing together? If we own it deeply, we will celebrate the victories but more importantly will feel the stresses and challenges of the process at a deep level? Ultimately, this depth of

purpose is fundamental to sustaining motivation when times inevitably get difficult.

As a startup technology company, it was critical for our small team to all feel a strong sense of ownership. In the hustle of the every day, we had to know and trust that each of us would do whatever it would take to make it work, to make the clients happy, to make the technology scalable, to make the business successful. We also had to have enough ownership to step up for each other when others needed to step back to take care of themselves. Ownership isn't just about doing more or having more accountability for tasks; it's about the whole and our being part of it. Ownership, therefore, should never be confused with the concept of buy-in. Buy-in is circumstantial and peripheral in that ownership belongs to someone else, so there is little-to-no loss when you sell out.

Commitment to Each Other

In many ways, commitment is the operational component to a personal sense of ownership. Commitment gets tested when things are rough, when people are stressed and work still has to get done. Who's got our back? Who's willing to do what it takes? Who sees and is invested in my personal success as fundamental to overall success? This can be in a sports team facing a comeback, a family at a critical time, a classroom commitment to learning, a startup being a startup. It is a commitment to our shared purpose and trying to make it happen specifically with and through each other. Nobody goes rogue.

This idea, like many, is most obvious when it breaks down. When I was in business school, we were organized in teams for the two years. For the first several months, the work was mostly individual and the team was there to help each other out, to share in each other's experiences and knowledge bases. This is how I made it through Accounting! Each individual, however, turned in his own assignment and got his own grade and so forth. During this time, our team got along great!

Then, most of the work for the rest of the two years changed into group work and the "shit hit the fan" as they say. Those initial months had clearly built some commitments among sets of people within the team, but not among the team as a whole. I'll spare the gory details, but people couldn't and wouldn't make meetings; people didn't collaborate or communicate. There was no shared commitment to each other's learning and success as part of the team's. So, in fact, there was no team.

Teaching/Learning
Teaching and learning are part of any creative relationship. We all have to realize that we have something important to share with the world, with each other, and, if we believe that, then others do too. One of my biggest challenges in my community work with youth was convincing them that I didn't have all the answers – or rather, that I KNEW I didn't have all the answers. It wasn't so much that they thought I did but

that they had spent too much time with adults who thought they did. It took months of me asking questions, intentionally making mistakes in front of them and vocally and openly accepting when I was wrong, thanking them when they taught me something, to finally establish this level of trust and tension.

One of the examples I have given over the years just to prove my discipline in breaking down this cultural power dynamic of adult as teacher and youth as learner was in my refusal to ever give them an answer for something they could find out for themselves. I wouldn't even provide the definition of a word if they asked. I responded with: where could you find that? That's why we ended up spending a year and a half with them researching for themselves the issues in and around college access – information they wanted to know and could find and articulate for themselves. That's why they wrote their own white paper on the issue. I could have knocked it all out on my own in two weeks. But the process, the learning, the relationships, the commitment building that went into them doing it for themselves was the goal. The process. It wasn't about information. It was about developing advocates and their shared purpose.

Once we shifted those ageist cultural dynamics, once we had some creative tension, we could work better as partners. We could have a more creative relationship as youth and adults.

Collective Action

Creative tension requires some action that depends on our relationships, not just you or me as effective individuals. We must create something together. I had a high school baseball coach who was so furious at us one game that, despite his being wheelchair bound and dying of cancer, he rolled up to us by the dugout and furiously, if weakly, gruffed: "You guys need to run back out to your positions and take a crap on them so you can tell your family you did something on the field today." I guess maybe this was his way of saying we had been ineffective in our collective action!?

Keeping on the sports theme, I have done consulting work for a number of years with a Special Olympics initiative called Project UNIFY. Project UNIFY works with teams of young people and adults to create more inclusive schools. When you work with groups like this with far reaching abilities, physical and mental, the sense of collective action is the driver of all you do. Any adult or young person without intellectual disabilities can go out and advocate for those with disabilities, tell the world how difficult life can be, how hurtful the R-word is, how bad it feels to be excluded and secluded in their schools. But, the power of the work comes when we all support those who experience these realities first hand in speaking for themselves. In doing so, we have to model for other young people and adults relationships built on creative tension – not charity or sympathy or altruism. That is how today's work gets done and how tomorrow's collective action for inclusion grows.

Group and Individual Reflection

It is very difficult to learn the most important lessons of our life and our work without stepping back to reflect. In the moment, we are too busy. Our emotions are too high. We are not objective. We are still experiencing it. So, reflection has to be intentional and has to have its own space and time to be meaningful. The process itself can be individual or group, formal or informal. All are valuable and in most cases all are needed at particular times.

Because formal and informal reflection are parts of everything I have done, I don't really have a specific example to share that is all that useful. But, over the years, I have found these three questions that you can ask yourself quietly or in a group to be a good place to start.

1. What did you learn from the experience?
2. What surprised you about the experience? (Bonus question: why?)
3. What still feels unresolved, or, what questions do you still have?

For a summary of these relational tension elements as both creative and destructive tension, see Figure 1.

Figure 1: Elements of Relational Tension

	Creative	**Destructive**
Shared purpose	Common goal that necessitates working together to accomplish	Many small goals owned individually attempting to support collective success
Ownership of work	The collective owns the goal and understands various roles, responsibilities, skills, and relationships needed to achieve the goal.	Ownership exists at the top and trickles down as directive, or is owned at the bottom and trickles up as misalignment.
Commitment to each other	All parties commit to the process of working together as part of their responsibilities and strategy in the work.	All parties focus only on doing their job rather than engaging the work of the whole.
Teaching/ Learning	Everyone is a teacher and a learner.	There are teachers and there are learners.
Collective action	The act of working together creates tension that informs the purpose and nature of the work in a generative way.	Individual actions taken based on responsibilities such that there is no generative tension created as part of action, but only the tension created by results.
Group and individual reflection	The collective remains vigilant and reflective, as individuals and as a group, so that the tension remains timely and creative.	Reflection does not happen among all parties. If it happens, it is at the individual level and does not inform or evolve the structure of the work.

Creative Tension vs. Destructive Tension

Before moving on, I want to play out the elements of relational tension in a brief case study related to planning that should feel pretty familiar to anyone who has worked in an organization, company, or with any collection of people trying to accomplish something. For continuity, I'm keeping it with the Project UNIFY theme for a little longer.

The following shows two possibilities for some relatively simply planning among school faculty to improve student outcomes. While this just illustrates the start of planning, the same models and considerations can be extended through all stages of action, reflection, assessment, and improvement. And, this example could easily be translated to a scenario with any business leader and her employees who are trying to plan anything. I'll trust you get the point without my having to do that for you.

Making a Plan: The Destructive Tension Approach
A principal is approached by a group of teachers who are concerned about his recently announced increased expectations for providing interventions and supports for students with intellectual disabilities. The new standards will be rolled out next semester. They are concerned, in particular, about not being given any additional planning time for new the strategies. The principal listened to their concerns and then explained the rationale he used to make his decision. He assured them it was the right decision for their school. He knew

they were "up to the task." The principal recommended that the teachers use their current individual prep time to collaborate with other staff and develop individualized plans to meet students' needs. He asked to see their plans at the next staff meeting.

Making a Plan: The Creative Tension Approach

A principal is approached by a group of teachers who are concerned about his recently announced increased expectations for providing interventions and supports for students with intellectual disabilities. The new standards will be rolled out next semester. They are concerned, in particular, about not being given any additional planning time for new the strategies. The principal adds this topic to the agenda of a staff meeting scheduled for the next week.

In that meeting, he asks staff to consider what each is doing in their classroom to ensure all learners have equitable access to instruction that meets their individual learning needs. (Reflection) Through the discussion, the staff begins to acknowledge that too many students are not finding success and that they as a staff collectively use a fairly narrow range of strategies. (Ownership)

Together with the principal, they agree on a shared goal to adopt a wider variety of interventions and supports to increase student success and identify the ones they want to focus on first and why. (Purpose) As part of this, they make a plan to have fellow teachers who are experts in the priority areas provide brief peer-to-peer professional development opportunities during each staff meeting. Over time, they have a vision that each teacher shares her successes and challenges with the group in such a professional development opportunity. (Commitment, Teaching/Learning)

The principal and staff develop a plan to allocate time for teachers to plan for implementation and engage a teacher coach to provide modeling and time to practice and refine their skills. (Collective Action)

The principal and staff schedule regular, frequent opportunities to reflect and refine practice individually, with the coach, and in professional learning communities. (Reflection)

To reduce the destructive tension that often undercuts efforts to improve how our schools or businesses function, intentional practices that nurture creative tension need to be imbedded in relationships throughout our organizations and systems. And, these relationships can't start when you need to get something done, or at a moment of urgency. They have to already be in place and then leveraged at that moment.

There are going to be times, as a leader, when we have to give a directive. That's part of being in a leadership position. But, if we have already built trust, if we have proven that we typically work with others to generate creative tension, people are much more likely to accept our directive. It just can't be our normal practice, or people will never own their work or commit to it even when we aren't around.

Marriage

In the spirit of reflection, I want to pause here and acknowledge that when I shared the very first draft of what became this book with my critical friend Terry Pickeral, he noted that I had talked about my relationships in work, with my community, as a son, a father, and seemingly everything else. But, I had not shared anything I have learned from being a husband. Aside from saying "thanks for the feedback" I was left thinking: "well, damn, what's that about!?"

I am pretty sure that response defines why we need critical friends in the first place! And, it's a sign I have a good one!

I thought for days about this feedback and tried to discern why I had never reflected publicly on this closest, most intimate, and most creative relationship in my life. And, ultimately, I think it's because I probably feel least secure about my role as a husband. That's a pretty hard thing to accept, honestly, much less to write about. Husband still feels like a role I don't know that much about, even as I have a loving, supportive, and patient spouse and 12 years of experience with it.

So, I reread my own writing here, and incredibly, everything about creative tension applies pretty seamlessly. If ever there were a relationship in which two people were holding opposite ends of a rubber band, it's marriage! Take a moment and re-read the elements of creative tension and think about your most important and intimate relationships – particularly those that have withstood the challenges of life and time. I realize my uncertainty as a husband is in part due to the fact that I have been less explicit in my marriage at calling these elements out as a point of process. I believe they are all there, but should probably check with my wife!

Here is another reality: my wife is not married to the man in 2015 she said "I do" to in 2003. I have grown and evolved and changed. I have been bruised and scarred physically and emotionally. I have taken on new roles and adapted to them: being a father, a student, an entrepreneur, an adult son and brother. Similarly, she has grown and changed and evolved. She could write her own version of this book. But, if my wife had somehow been the one woman on the planet specifically interested in marrying her ideal man with an art degree (with significant debt to show for it) and a $30,000 salary working with kids in a flooded church basement doing work no one could ever explain but the kids and me, she would be pretty upset a dozen years later! Neither of us is the same person we were then, and yet, we are equally committed to each other, continue to share our evolving goals, to teach and learn and reflect; and with two children, we are more focused on collective action than ever before!

Perhaps, therein is the lesson Terry was pushing me to identify. In marriage, in relationships, we have to iterate and create and recreate our selves and our relationship - independently. I must constantly invest in my own becoming. So must my wife. We both have to tend to our present and future selves with a sense of creative tension. That's the foundation of our ability to invest in each other with creative relational tension. "I" exist independently of "her" and "we" exist as a unique union of both. So, marriage is made up of three parts: I, You, and We. Each is unique and requires its own form of creative tension to stay healthy.

Creative Leadership

Clearly, not every relationship has the same commitment or context as marriage. So, in less personal and less intimate relationships, how do we lead creatively? How do we cultivate creative tension that allows us to build relationships in the first place? How do we maintain high levels of productivity, effectiveness, and engagement through those relationships? How do we lead in a way that capitalizes on the abilities, experiences, and perspectives of our people? Here are some thoughts to get started:

1. Promote and celebrate questions and all that comes with them.

I've already discussed the importance of questions pretty extensively, so here I am really focused on the implications of being open to questions and how to do that well and responsibly. The worst thing I can do as a leader is talk as if I want people's ideas and then ignore them when I get them. This is worse than never pretending to be open at all; I go from asshole to dishonest, disingenuous asshole pretty quickly. Inviting people's questions and opinions as a leader is about listening and relationship building, not just about doing what they ask. Leaders often fear opening themselves to these expectations – some use it as an excuse - but most people know this.

People want to be heard. So, that means I am open to their ideas and respectful of their questions and I take the time to acknowledge, appreciate, and respond – whether I agree or not. It also means that I am intentional about promoting and communicating when someone's question prompts critical reflection or helps me think differently about the work we are doing together. If I publicly acknowledge people for their questions and insights I will build my influence as a leader even as I increase their sense of power and ownership. It can be a profound dynamic with just the slightest bit of intentionality and humility.

A creative relationship, like any relationship, is two-way and the communication upon which that relationship is built also has to be two-ways. If only certain people get to ask questions, have opinions, generate ideas, or give answers and others do not then I cannot build a creative, learning organization. Teaching and learning and questioning have to be modeled and encouraged and respected at all levels and abilities.

2. Understand and embrace change.

"If you don't like change, you're going to like irrelevance even less." - General Eric Shinseki

There are plenty of books and articles already out there about how to manage change. What I want to focus on instead is a deeper understanding of the concept so that we can be more effective at leading it. What is change? How do people deal with it? How should we talk about it?

To lead change, we must first understand the magnitude of change we expect or need. We must also recognize that the sense of magnitude is largely defined by how the individuals we really need to co-lead and implement that change perceive the demands on them. Understanding their perception of the change is the only way we can share ownership with them to co-lead it. Even if we believe the change we need is organizational (not individual), we can never forget that an organization is just a bunch of individuals! That's the reality when it comes to implementation anyway. So, are we asking those individuals to develop new skills? Are we creating new processes and procedures that they will have to adapt to? Is the change structural and requiring major shifts in formal and informal relationships and power dynamics? Are we attempting to change our culture and unearthing and undoing unspoken norms and behaviors that have never been questioned? Needless to say, developing new skills and shifting culture represent significantly different magnitudes of change.

The magnitude will determine our timeline, our strategies, and who we need on our leadership team to make it happen. The fact is that most change efforts don't work, or at least don't fully achieve the initially intended outcome. There is a change model out of Harvard that may shed some light on these challenges. The model says that:

Change = Dissatisfaction x Vision x Plan

Why is this simple model so powerful? At the simplest level, what happens when you have a zero for any of these elements? No change.

It's basic multiplication, but profound in that so many of our traditional change efforts are built on addition strategies. If we do this and then we get that then it will add up to change. If we add this resource…If we add this position…If we add this new frame for our work…

Addition alone doesn't generate real change. Change is multiplicative. The elements necessary for change are interdependent and exponential magnifiers of each other. If we want to lead change, we must understand the whole concept. We must invest the time, energy, and effort to turn dissatisfaction into creative energy, to use it to build a shared vision, and capture it in a plan to deliver the change you collectively want and need. The obvious implication then, which may seem counterintuitive, is that as a leader I may have to invest in cultivating some carefully crafted dissatisfaction. Sometimes that's what I need to do to generate the energy for a new vision.

3. See the work and organization as fundamentally a network of relationships.

Everyone knows the old saying that "perception is reality." Sadly, most of us have become attuned to it as a trite response to some interpersonal dissonance rather than a deep, strategic way of understanding the world around us. While this could be a broad ranging conversation and perhaps even a book unto itself, I want to frame it by continuing the discussion of change. When I was working with youth, I had colleagues who did a lot of work with youth in foster care, kids who had transitioned in and out of families and systems literally all of their lives. In their advocacy for improving those systems, they also did a lot of education of lawmakers and other influential people in the system. Much of it was founded on a basic understanding of William Bridges' Transitions Model.

Change affects people differently and people respond at different paces over time. But, there are some consistent patterns that, if we understand them, we may recognize when we face the inevitable resistance to change. If we can recognize where people are with our change efforts, where they are personally in the transition, we may be better at communicating with them and bringing them along.

Perhaps most fundamentally, we need to understand that change means that something is ending. That's where most people start, whether they can articulate it or not. Someone for whom the status quo is working is about to lose something. According to Bridges, people go through a whole range of emotions triggered by change that initially manifest as destructive tension but can, with effective leadership, transform to creative tension. His model suggests that people transition from a sense of an ending through denial and anger then fear, confusion and stress before they reach a sort of disillusioned low point where they try to avoid the issue altogether. Clearly, this is a non-linear process unique to individuals, but identifying the pattern and where we, or our people, are is the point.

If we can help people get out of avoidance and move forward into a space of healthy skepticism, impatience, and even creativity, then we have the opportunity to generate hope and enthusiasm for a new beginning. All this is to say, change is often complex and emotional, so managing our relationships is fundamental to our success.

To get there though, we must communicate with our people - constantly. More importantly, we have to communicate with them in a way that they can hear and understand, which again means we have to have some understanding of where they are emotionally related to the change we are trying to implement. Social Judgment Theory focuses on this kind of communication and talks about three domains, or latitudes, that our message can fall into for the recipients: the latitude of acceptance, latitude of non-commitment, and latitude of resistance. As leaders, we have to craft our messages with an understanding of what our recipients are ready and able to hear. This is not only about framing and tweaking language, but also about how much information we share, when, and how quickly. It's not about manipulation, just smart, effective communication. It's about knowing people's junk and speaking to it, through it, or around it, whichever is needed at a given time.

4. Invite feedback often and give feedback well.

"To be curious about how someone else interprets things, we have to be willing to admit that we're not capable of figuring things out alone. If our solutions don't work as well as we want them to, if our explanations of why something happened don't feel sufficient, it's time to begin asking others about what they see and think. When so many interpretations are available, I can't understand why we would be satisfied with superficial conversations where we pretend to agree with one another." – Margaret Wheatley[47]

The fact is that there is no reality, no single truth, in our organizations. "There exists no pure, uninterpreted datum; all facts embody theory"[48] and are colored by an individual's perceptions, beliefs, and their experiences in the social order of the organization. So, the point of feedback is to expose the multiplicity of truths that are driving behavior and decisions throughout our organization. Feedback is also another form of

---

[47] Wheatley, Margaret J. *Turning to One Another: Simple Conversations to Restore Hope to the Future.* San Francisco: Berrett-Koshler Publishers, Inc., 2002
[48] Anderson, Walter Truett. "Themes of Postmodernity." *The Truth about the Truth: De-confusing and Re-constructing the Postmodern World.* New York: Putnam, 1995. 19. Print.

communication and opportunity for relationship building.

So, as leaders, we have to be particularly mindful that we are not always the ones giving feedback and asking others to receive it, just as we can't always be the ones asking the questions or giving answers. As part of our leadership strategy then, we need to create explicit opportunities where we receive feedback, openly, publicly, and honestly. If we can't receive it in such a way then why would we expect others to? This again is where modeling is fundamental to leadership.

But, let's also be honest here: if we open ourselves to feedback we're going to hear some shit, and, we are going to catch some shit. It might get a bit uncomfortable. It too is risky. Guess what: that's my job as a creative leader! Taking on such risks openly is how we will generate creative tension, build our culture, and share ownership of our vision of with our people.

"Since the artist cares in a peculiar way for the phase of experience in which union is achieved, he does not shun moments of resistance and tension. He rather cultivates them, not for their own sake, but for their potentialities..."[49]

We have to know as leaders that these times of dissonance are the source of creativity in our organization or company. They are what create "potentialities" and drive growth and improvement. We also have to know that just as most of our ideas are "shite" most of theirs are too! We just don't ever let them

---

[49] Dewey, John. *Art as Experience*. New York: Minton, Balch, 1934. 14. Print.

know we know that, or we will never hear the good ones. Our job is to listen to all of them, grab the good ones, run with them, and give our people highly visible credit for them. This, in turn, will inspire people to speak up with more good feedback in a virtuous cycle.

5. Celebrate and recognize success at all levels.
As organizations grow from startup to business, from grassroots to institution, the largely horizontal founding relationships give way to and get complicated by the necessary vertical responsibilities that "organize" them. And, as this happens, not only does the space between the "top and bottom" of the organization expand, those relationships also get more distant. Further, as more people take on more specific, functional roles, the ability for each to see his role and importance to the whole becomes increasingly difficult.

Our job as leaders is to never let our people lose sight of the value they provide. Whether that's a janitor, a data wonk, an administrative assistance, an analyst or whoever, we have to acknowledge and celebrate their contributions. Similarly, we must find ways to celebrate not just people fulfilling their roles but their unique skills and perspectives that they bring to our collective work. We have to be inclusive as we celebrate, and this takes practice and discipline – not to mention a deep understanding of our people and our work. But, again, that's my job as a leader.

And finally, for leaders, it all comes back to seeing the whole. General Stanley McChrystal summarizes: "The primary responsibility of the new leader is to maintain a holistic, big-picture view, avoiding a reductionist approach, no matter how tempting micromanaging may be. Perhaps an organization sells widgets, and the leader finds that he or she loves *everything* about widgets – designing, building, and marketing them; that's still not where the leader is most needed. The leader's first responsibility is to the *whole*."[50]

---

[50] McChrystal, Stanley A., and Tantum Collins. *Team of Teams: New Rules of Engagement for a Complex World.* New York: Penguin Group, 2015. 232. Print.

CLOSING

"Go out in the world and fuck it up beautifully." - John Waters[51]

"To be changed is the destiny of all meanings we produce. One should speak in order to generate a dialogue. We must abandon this absurd desire to be fully understood or to express the truth. No one speaks in order to express the truth. One should speak in order to provoke a response, so truth can be heard together."
- Alexander M. Sidorkin[52]

Art is iterative. The learning process is iterative. Life is iterative. Creating requires putting out incomplete ideas, incomplete selves, testing hypotheses, and accepting that they are just that: incomplete, hypotheses. It requires honest critique without judgment. It requires growing into the possibility of what's next rather than stagnating in what is or was.

So, to remain artists, learners, creators, and innovators, to remain truly living, means that we can't judge an iteration as if it were a final conclusion. We don't judge the seedling for not being a flower. We don't judge the child for not being an adult. Instead, we cultivate and observe and adapt as change happens and as we identify new needs and strategies for development.

Similarly, when creating a new product, offering a new service, or even just sharing a new idea, we need to

---

[51] https://www.youtube.com/watch?v=Hl05XGifKb4
[52] Sidorkin, Alexander. *Learning Relations Impure Education, Deschooled Schools, & Dialogue with Evil.* Peter Lang International Academic, 2002. 170. Print.

understand each iteration as a point in a process, in progress, rather than a singular point for finite evaluation. We cannot judge each stroke of a painting as if it were the finished product. We will become paralyzed. We will constantly solve problems and someday realize we never created the new reality we started out working for. When we look at yesterday's work through the eyes and knowledge of today, it can seem woefully inadequate. It should. That's because we have learned. But again, judging rather than creating on this moment would be like saying the first step on a ladder is a failure because it doesn't get us to the top.

At the end of the day, we only fail when we stop iterating, when we stop becoming. And, we typically only stop becoming when 1. We stop learning, 2. We fear failure, 3. We don't care anymore.

So, our products and art and selves should always be incomplete.

If they weren't, what would we create?

For more about the author or to read additional essays on art, business, education, and life, please visit:

www.andersonwwilliams.com

Made in the USA
Charleston, SC
20 March 2016